Paracelsus

and

Other One-Act Plays

D1192997

Studies in Austrian Literature, Culture, and Thought

Translation Series

ARTHUR SCHNITZLER

Paracelsus

and Other One-Act Plays

Translated by G. J. Weinberger

Afterword by Herbert Lederer

ARIADNE PRESS

Ariadne Press would like to express its appreciation to the Austrian
Cultural Institute, New York and the Austrian Ministry of Education
and Art, Vienna for their assistance in publishing this book.

Library of Congress Cataloging-in-Publication Data

Schnitzler, Arthur, 1862-1931.
    [Plays. English. Selections]
    Paracelsus and other one-act plays / Arthur Schnitzler ;
translated by G.J. Weinberger ; afterword by Herbert Lederer.
        p.   cm. -- (Studies in Austrian literature, culture,
and thought. Translation series)
    Contents: Paracelsus -- The green cockatoo -- Marionettes
-- The puppeteer -- The gallant Cassian -- The great puppet
show -- The transformation of Pierrot -- The veil of Pierrette.
    ISBN 0-929497-96-1
    I. Weinberger, G.J. II. Title. III. Series.
PT2638.N5A28 1995
833'.8--dc20   94-21539
                                                              CIP

Cover Design:
Art Director: George McGinnis
Designer, Illustrator: David Hubbell

Copyright ©1995
by Ariadne Press
270 Goins Court
Riverside, CA 92507

For Jill

". . . weil nie meine Sehnsucht vergeht."

CONTENTS

ACKNOWLEDGMENTS

I wish particularly to thank my friend, Herbert Lederer, Professor Emeritus at the University of Connecticut, for his help and encouragement in the preparation of these translations, especially for his many valuable suggestions regarding *Paracelsus*. An instrumental part of the Schnitzler-Renaissance of the 1950s and thereafter, Professor Lederer set a standard of sound scholarship and clear writing for those who have come after him. I am both grateful and proud that he agreed to write the Afterword for the present volume.

New Britain, Connecticut
September, 1993

TRANSLATOR'S NOTE

Of the seven plays presented here, four appear in English for the first time. Of the others, *Paracelsus* and *The Gallant Cassian* have been available only in versions which must now strike the reader as outdated and, apparently, hastily written. *The Green Cockatoo*, in contrast, has been translated a number of times, most recently by Paul F. Dvorak, whose version appears in his *Illusion and Reality. Plays and Stories of Arthur Schnitzler*, published by Peter Lang in 1986. I decided to include my own translation of this play in the present volume for thematic reasons similar to those Professor Dvorak must have had in mind: no collection of Schnitzler's one-act plays dealing with illusion and reality would be complete without *The Green Cockatoo*.

I was concerned, naturally, that translations done within a few years of each other might resemble each other a good deal. And, indeed, although I avoided reading Professor Dvorak's until after I had completed and revised my own, our respective efforts are very often similar and, at times, identical. This is unavoidable: his translation is good, as I hope my own is, and we share a common language.

PARACELSUS

Verse Play in One Act

CHARACTERS

CYPRIAN, *an armorer*

JUSTINA, *his wife*

CECILIA, *his sister*

DOCTOR COPUS, *town doctor*

ANSELM, *a young nobleman*

THEOPHRASTUS BOMBAST HOHENHEIM,
   called Paracelsus

*The action takes place at Cyprian's house in Basel,
on a beautiful June morning at the beginning of
the sixteenth century.*

The well-furnished room has two doors, the one on the left
leading to Justina's room, the other into the anteroom.

FIRST SCENE

JUSTINA *is sitting at the window, busy at the spinning wheel.*
CECILIA *enters.*
JUSTINA *looking up, calmly*
  What? Back so soon?
CECILIA   It's too noisy in town.
  She sits down
  My head hurts; I had to come home again.
  Had you been with me in the market place,
  You'd have come back as well.
JUSTINA   Why's that?
CECILIA   Because
  There's such a crowding and rude shouting there
  As no sane person can long tolerate.
JUSTINA Anything to see? Any new conjurers?
CECILIA Hasn't the maid told you?
JUSTINA   She's not back yet.
CECILIA Of course; she won't be coming home today.
  All Basel, I believe, is spellbound there.
  They all flock to the spot; and there they stand
  As if great miracles were to be seen.
JUSTINA What sort of miracles, you mixed-up thing?
CECILIA There is a quack — nothing more.
JUSTINA   That's not much!
CECILIA That's what I said. We've had more than enough

Odd fellows of that kind in our city.
What do they find so special about this one?
JUSTINA Must be a famous, widely-traveled one —
Didn't you hear his name? —
CECILIA   A lot of names
Whizzed by me — but I've forgotten them all.
Praise God I'm home — my head is still spinning.

SECOND SCENE

Justina, Cecilia. Doctor Copus enters.

COPUS I bid you good morrow, worthy ladies.
JUSTINA
I'm glad you've come; *smiling* the child is ill again.
COPUS Then she's the first who waits for me today,
For everyone else ran away from me.
JUSTINA Where are they?
COPUS   Where —? Why, in the marketplace!
Paracelsus has appeared to us, you know,
What further need for Doctor Copus?
CECILIA   Right!
Paracelsus was his name!
JUSTINA   Paracelsus?
It's him then! The most famous of all doctors!
COPUS *angrily* What's that? Most famous?
CECILIA *appeasing him*   She didn't mean it.
COPUS And "Doctor" —? Please — call me an unknown quack
If Paracelsus is either famous
Or a doctor!

CECILIA *almost anxiously* What then is he?
COPUS   A fraud.
  Enough of that now.— *Breaks off* How are you, dear Miss?
  Takes Cecilia's pulse.
  A bit fast.
CECILIA   I have a fever, don't I?
COPUS   Did you take your medicine this morning?
CECILIA   Of course; as you prescribed, Doctor Copus.
  And even so, my pulse is still too fast?
COPUS   "Even so"! Had you not taken your pill
  It would go twice as quickly.
CECILIA   Shall I take
  One more today?
COPUS   Your tongue now, if you please.
  Cecilia sticks out her tongue.
COPUS   Not bad, Miss. It should only remain so.
CECILIA   But my head is worse than in a long time.
COPUS   *without listening to her, suddenly furious again.*
  And you know who's down there like other folk?
JUSTINA   Who? — And where?—
COPUS   Master Cyprian is standing
  In the market listening to the swindler.
JUSTINA   My husband?
COPUS   Yes, he, who else scorns rabble,
  The homeless sort, who roam from street to street,
  Stands in the square — no! on the very steps
  Leading up to Paracelsus's platform.
  And hears and sees, and wonders, and goes crazy!
JUSTINA   But tell me now, what is so wonderful
  About this man?
COPUS   I find only one thing
  Wonderful: his tremendous impudence.

Here's one remark I heard with my own ears:
My beard alone has more and deeper learning
Than all doctors and scribblers together.
JUSTINA Sounds like a joke!—
COPUS   Oh sure, just take his side!
He mocks Avicenna! Scoffs at Galen!
Casts aspersion on all who've come before
And who've brought our exalted craft so far.
He laughs at the school he himself comes from,
Reviles physicians and apothecaries.
And what do you think this shameless fellow does
In order to enchant our honest people?—
The potions and medicines which sick folk
Have brought him, these he pours out on the ground
And heaves the bottles into the distance,
And simply blows the powders in the air,
And shouts thereto: What once Hippocrates
Was, that and more am I, I, Paracelsus!
And your physicians are dull simpletons!
JUSTINA And Cyprian is standing there?
COPUS   And listens!
And half of Basel gawks in amazement,
My own patients I saw there, awaiting
His diagnosis.
CECILIA   He's seeing patients?
COPUS Would you like to see for yourself, maybe?
Yes, he's seeing them; if you don't believe it,
Tomorrow's death roll will give proof enough.
But I would rather say to you, farewell.
I'm off to City Hall, I'm resigning
My position — and want to spend my scant
Remnant of life far from thankless Basel.

CECILIA But Doctor! — And my head? What shall I do?
COPUS Let me show you how that swindler does it.
JUSTINA Yes, please, do show us.
CECILIA   You intend to use
  That man's methods to experiment on me?
COPUS What, Miss, your head hurts?
CECILIA   Ah, but you know that.
COPUS I'm speaking as Paracelsus; pay heed!
  Now look at me!
  He stares at her, makes hypnotizing motions with his hands.
                  Your headache's disappeared.
CECILIA It's still here — and more intense than ever.
COPUS That's how he does it: without medicines —
  And he insults those who do otherwise.
  And that is his widely-praised artistry.
  And all this in Basel; inconceivable!
JUSTINA I would think he acts the same everywhere.
COPUS Of course, but it was here that he still sat
  At his master's feet thirteen years ago.
  He was Trithemius's student! Don't you know?
JUSTINA Trithemius? the doctor who died last year?
COPUS In good time too! and to this same city,
  After roaming through the entire world,
  Through Sweden, Prussia, and all Tartary,
  Moving from one town to the next — fleeing —
  Understand me well: he had cause to flee —
  He now comes back, to this city, that taught
  The ABCs of that most noble art
  Which he's forgotten, which he now denies.
JUSTINA Tell me, who is he? He lived in Basel?
COPUS You knew him well, when he was still simply
  Bombastus Theophrastus Hohenheim —

JUSTINA *highly excited*
  What did you say? Theophrastus . . .
COPUS   Hohenheim.
JUSTINA That's him?
COPUS   Yes, him.
JUSTINA   The great Paracelsus,
  Do you hear, Cecilia, is Hohenheim,
  Of whom I told you.
CECILIA   But what's the matter?
JUSTINA You didn't know him — you were still a child —
  But now I know why Cyprian is listening.

THIRD SCENE

Cecilia, Justina, Copus. Anselm enters.

ANSELM You didn't hear my knocking — hence, I beg
  Your pardon for entering unannounced.
  — Do I interrupt? The Master's not here?
JUSTINA Not yet.
ANSELM *affected, but amiably*
                    How is the loveliest of ladies?
  And how the most charming of young maidens?
  And how the most learned of gentlemen?
CECILIA And how the most unbearable of knights?
ANSELM *without taking his eyes from Justina*
  Not well at all — for soon must he depart
  This fair city and much that he holds dear.
CECILIA Are you sure now? — You've promised many times!

ANSELM My father summons me. I must go home,
  Before *Glances at Justina* I reach the goal of my desire.
  Master Thomas is still not satisfied:
  I play the organ badly; I can't grasp
  Composition — and I've not completed
  A single song of all that I've begun.
CECILIA The reason is simple.
COPUS   You're still too young,
  And music is a hard, demanding art.
ANSELM Everything's hard for an unhappy man.
CECILIA And one who carouses the whole night through,
  And rolls the dice until the break of dawn,
  Has never yet succeeded properly
  At anything by light of day.
JUSTINA *reproachfully*   Cecilia!
COPUS That's how you carry on? That is not good.
ANSELM Have you any cure for a grieving soul?
COPUS It isn't dice.
ANSELM   Nor is it wine, either.
  Yet both grant forgetfulness — that is good.
COPUS I'm not your doctor — hence I must not speak.
CECILIA But you are mine — and look, my head still hurts
  And I'm standing here, helpless.
COPUS   Forgive me,
  Miss, I'll prescribe for you immediately
  Something that will help you within the hour.
CECILIA Come up to my room, Doctor.
COPUS   By your leave.
  Copus and Cecilia exit.

FOURTH SCENE

Justina, Anselm

ANSELM Justina!

JUSTINA   Hush!

ANSELM   Today you ask in vain!
   That I must leave Basel is true; and true
   That I see you today for the last time,
   And I have to tell you —

JUSTINA   I won't hear it.

ANSELM Then I'll keep still — but let my silence speak.

JUSTINA Every single word of yours insults me,
   And your every glance offends my honor.

ANSELM These glances, that look up as to a goddess,
   These words, ascending, much like a prayer —

JUSTINA Enough, I say!

ANSELM   You don't know me, Justina,
   You don't know what I want — scarce what I am.
   You take me for a fool — or a bungler!
   I'm neither! I am more than you suspect.
   What maims my gifts of spirit is that you
   Don't recognize them and despise them all.
   A mere smile from those lips could make an artist
   Of me — a kiss transform me to a master!

JUSTINA *having regained her composure, she is cool and
sharp*
   Go find what you need to work somewhere else.
   I have neither kisses nor smiles to give.

ANSELM I would sing the most wonderful songs, then,
   In praise of my dearly beloved mistress,
   And we would reach posterity as one.

JUSTINA The blush of youth has never seduced me —
  And shall fame — a mere shadow, tempt me now?
  Look here — you've asked of me only a smile. . .
  I'll give you more. . .
ANSELM   Oh speak!
JUSTINA   I'll laugh out loud. *Laughs.*
ANSELM You are driving me mad.
JUSTINA   The road is long.
ANSELM And death its end. . .
JUSTINA   We all must pass that way.
ANSELM *throws himself down before her*
  At your feet I implore you, come tonight
  To your garden — I want to press my lips
  Upon your hands there, one last time. There's none
  Will see us. I will climb over the fence. . .
  The night is discreet. I'll wait in the arbor. . .
JUSTINA You're mad. . . Get up. My husband is coming.
ANSELM What does it matter? If he should see me
  On my knees before you, he'd only laugh —
  So cheerfully does he stroll through the world,
  So sure of his wife and so besotted
  With proud joy of exclusive possession —
  But I tell you: this sort of presumption. . .
JUSTINA Do stand up — for God's sake — can't you hear —

FIFTH SCENE

Anselm, Justina, Cyprian. Later Paracelsus

CYPRIAN *smiling at the others' confusion*
  My dear young squire, are you here again?

ANSELM I am. . . I only wanted —

CYPRIAN *without paying attention to him, to Justina*
My dear child,
I'm bringing a marvelous guest today
With whom we'll have our bit of amusement.
Justina is slightly alarmed.
My dearest Paracelsus, please come in.
Paracelsus appears at the door.
A simple, middle-class house — still, I think,
It won't seem too bad to one accustomed
To sleeping under the stars.

PARACELSUS Worthy Master,
Heaven's canopy ought not be despised.

CYPRIAN *pointing to Anselm*
Meet Anselm, a young noble, in Basel
To learn to play the organ. . . the organ, right?

ANSELM Yes, I want to learn to play the organ.

CYPRIAN *remembering*
With Master Thomas. . . of course. . . I supplied
Some splendid armaments to his father,
When he rode through here with his cavalry.
Shaking his head The father a warrior. . . a musician
The son.

ANSELM A pastime.

CYPRIAN Right. *To Paracelsus* Now, my good man,
We bid you welcome. After a long time
You'll spend an hour again in honest
Company with a cup of goodly wine.

PARACELSUS And does your pretty wife still recognize me?

JUSTINA Of course I do —

PARACELSUS *looks at her a long time*

CYPRIAN Well, he does look somewhat

Weatherbeaten for his years! Imagine,
The man cloaked in darkness and secrecy,
Whom wild tales precede like a mad herald,
This master sorcerer is Hohenheim,
Whom we knew in his pious student days.

PARACELSUS I'm no master sorcerer, dear lady.
Just a doctor who's smarter than the rest.

CYPRIAN We all know what doctors are, my good man.
They do not carry on with pranks like yours.
Still, whatever you are, you amuse me,
And since you've crossed my threshold, you're my guest —
No matter where you may be coming from.
I'm also pleased I always recognized
You for what you are, back then, years ago,
When you lived here in Basel, studying
Alchemy with Trithem, and reveling
In front of certain windows every night —
I knew: no good would ever come of you!

The maid enters with the wine; after placing it on the table she exits again; Justina busies herself at the table a little. Paracelsus observes Anselm attentively.

PARACELSUS Do you think so?

CYPRIAN   But this is my motto:
Let everyone live as it pleases him!
Where would be the merit in remaining
At one's own hearth, serving both the private
And the general good, carrying on
One's honest labors as a citizen,
If there were no others tempted to roam
Through the world as itinerant fellows?
At times I enjoy seeing such odd fish,
Who bring the savor from distant journeys.

For, one is thrice glad when they leave again
That he still has his home, his wife, his craft.
JUSTINA Your guest is still standing.
CYPRIAN   Please, do sit down,
And you, dear squire —
ANSELM   You will excuse me.
I have to go now; I'm leaving tonight.
CYPRIAN What?
ANSELM   Yes, my father calls and urges haste.
I've much to do before my departure.
I'll come at noon to bid you all farewell.
As he is leaving
I could tolerate that glance no longer.

SIXTH SCENE

Cyprian, Justina, Paracelsus

CYPRIAN What ails the youth?
JUSTINA *embarrassed*   I don't know.
CYPRIAN *laughing*   But I do!
I'll wager he spoke to you about love.
JUSTINA Not so.
CYPRIAN   And that you got angry —
JUSTINA   No — no.
CYPRIAN And sent him back home again with harsh words.
JUSTINA What can you be thinking?
CYPRIAN *laughing*   I hope you did.
JUSTINA Of course, I would have.
CYPRIAN   Look, how red she turns.
PARACELSUS And so confused, as if beauty were sin!

JUSTINA *almost in tears*
  I beg you. . . .
CYPRIAN *to Paracelsus* See, she hasn't changed.
PARACELSUS *with emphasis*   I see.
CYPRIAN *in jest* And is ashamed of her silent power,
  Which everyone who comes near her must feel.
  Well, you could sing a song on that score too.
JUSTINA *pleading*
  I beg you!
PARACELSUS Do memories frighten you?
  One can't remove their sting any better
  Than by recalling them to life again.
CYPRIAN Who here is frightened? The past is the past.
  She took me to be her husband, not you,
  And gives thanks daily to God for this choice.
  This house is mine, as it was my father's
  And my ancestors' for three hundred years.
  Its wealth increases through diligent work.
  Yes, indeed — look at me, my friend, this arm,
  Which, it's well known, has ample skill to forge
  A goodly sword and, should the need arise,
  To wield it as well, is more than suited
  Too for the task of shielding a woman.
  That's what a woman wants, and thus it is
  I won her; thus it is I can keep her.
  I have nothing to fear. . . not memories
  Nor any rapture of yours. A woman
  Is enclosed and held fast by the present.
  My door stands open wide. . . I fear no man.
PARACELSUS I wish these words were true as they are proud.
CYPRIAN I grant your wish — consider it fulfilled.

SEVENTH SCENE

*Justina, Cyprian, Paracelsus. Cecilia enters. When she
sees Paracelsus she starts to leave.*

CYPRIAN No, stay! This is Cecilia.
PARACELSUS   Your sister!
CYPRIAN She was still a mere child when you left town.
  Cecilia, this is a wonder-healer.
CECILIA I saw you earlier. . .
CYPRIAN   What do you think,
     Paracelsus, why not try your skill on her?
CECILIA How. . . What?
CYPRIAN   You just stay with us, and I'll bet
  The man can make you well with his magic.
PARACELSUS What did you say? "Magic"?
CYPRIAN   What other name
  Fits what I saw in the market today?
JUSTINA But now I want to see myself, at last,
  What it is that you can do.
CYPRIAN   Now she finds
  Her voice. Astonishment took it away —
  Curiosity restores it back again.
  In a condescending tone
  Of all the mountebanks who've appeared here,
  This is the one who brings his tricks off best.
  I don't care much for the type otherwise;
  These fire-eaters, snake-oil sellers, quacks,
  Alchemists and comedians aren't my cup
  Of tea. You are all scoundrels, after all.
PARACELSUS Possibly. Town councilors we're surely not.
CYPRIAN Your joke is saucy; still, I forgive you,

Because I am in good spirits today,
And because you know more than the others.
One can tell you learned something years ago,
And behind all the fraud you perpetrate,
Something like erudition flashes forth.

PARACELSUS *scornfully*

You jest!

CYPRIAN Listen, children, to what he did.

PARACELSUS Leave it alone. . .

CYPRIAN   Only what comes to mind.

To Justina and Cecilia

You know the blacksmith's wife?

CECILIA   The crippled one.

CYPRIAN She's been moving arms and legs since morning,
And what the others' efforts never managed,
This fellow here accomplished in an instant.

CECILIA Can it be?

CYPRIAN   There's still stranger stuff to tell.
Do you know the turner's little daughter?

JUSTINA Who suddenly became dumb this past winter?

CYPRIAN She speaks again, since he commanded her.

JUSTINA How is all this possible?

CYPRIAN   Sorcery!
And I've asked myself in some amazement,
How you've escaped the pyre until now.

PARACELSUS Patience, esteemed Master, time brings counsel.

CYPRIAN However, what perplexes me the most
Is what you did with Medardus.

Explaining   He made
The young man sink into a deep slumber
Just through the power of his eyes.

CECILIA   Your eyes?

CYPRIAN Then he says to him — we all could hear it —:
    You're coming home from a lengthy journey
    Through foreign lands, where you've experienced much.
    Do tell us all about it.
JUSTINA   And —?
CYPRIAN   He told!
JUSTINA Of people and of things he never saw?
CYPRIAN And of adventures that he never had.
JUSTINA And thought them true?
PARACELSUS   No longer than I wished
    Him to. I extinguished these dreams again
    And he no longer knows what he told us.
CYPRIAN And just you, yourself, could take what you gave.
PARACELSUS Certainly!
CYPRIAN   And if you had not freed him
    From these dreams, which you created in him?
PARACELSUS For the rest of his life he'd swear they're true.
    Stands up; suddenly in a different tone, almost with pathos
    That much can I do! Who can do as much?
    I can be fate itself, if I desire!
CYPRIAN That works but in the marketplace, my friend,
    Here you can skip the big talk, if you please.
    Fate comes from God, not from some sorcerer,
    And your work is delusion — but not truth.
PARACELSUS
    More than mere truth, which was and which shall be,
    Delusion exists now. . . The moment rules!
    If you could unroll the years of your life
    Just like a manuscript before your eyes,
    You'd scarcely be able to interpret
    A single page, because our memories
    Deceive almost as much as do our hopes —

Everything's mysterious. . . the minutes past
Like all succeeding ones! Only the moment
Is ours, and it's already gliding off.
Think about it: every night compels us
To descend into an alien region,
Depriving us of our strength and riches.
And all life's fullness and our gains therefrom
Don't have nearly the power of the dreams
That enter our defenseless sleep each night.

CYPRIAN I also have had my share of nightmares;
But what of it, one wakes again, you know,
The sun returns, as do the sounds of day,
One laughs at dreams and goes about his work.
Only a man who strives for naught, like you,
Can let himself be misled by a dream.
For men like me, who know what we want, fate
Is only what shows itself in daylight
And doesn't fade when we open our eyes.
Of course, the likes of you would gladly blur
The clear boundaries between day and night
And place us in twilight and doubtfulness.
Thanks be to God! There are some certainties:
A man like me still stands on solid ground,
Pious and strong, holds what is his secure.
Believe me, we're not afraid of your ilk.

PARACELSUS Nor is that required. — Still, you wanted
Me to cure your esteemed sister's ailment.

CYPRIAN Quite right.

CECILIA   I'm healthy. . . and have a doctor.

CYPRIAN Let Justina tell you, she trusts her more
Than she does me.

JUSTINA   She's in an ill humor.

Almost melancholy.
CECILIA   No.
JUSTINA   At times she sighs.
  And I've already seen tears in her eyes.
PARACELSUS And no one knows why?
CECILIA   I don't ever cry.
PARACELSUS My noble Miss — I will ask you nothing,
  Nor delve into the causes of your sorrow.
  I can take all your pains away from you,
  Even without your telling me their source.
CECILIA No, no —
CYPRIAN   I think yes, I'd like to hear it.
PARACELSUS A doctor's questions are often troubling,
  I'll spare you, and still restore you to health.
CECILIA And remove all my hurt?
PARACELSUS   That I will do.
CECILIA And I'll be wholly free then?
PARACELSUS   From all pain.
CECILIA And be merry?
PARACELSUS   You'll laugh the whole day long,
  Forgetting that you were ever troubled.
CECILIA No, no, I don't want to laugh and be merry.
CYPRIAN Will someone look at this fool of a girl —
  As if laughter weren't God's greatest blessing!
PARACELSUS If you'd prefer not to laugh, Miss, perhaps
  We could leave it at quiet cheerfulness.
CECILIA I don't want to be cheerful.
CYPRIAN   You don't want to?
JUSTINA What do you want, then?
CECILIA   To be left in peace.
PARACELSUS It seems, my child, the hurt oppressing you
  Is so suffused with youthful happiness

That you'd not miss it for all the world. Hence
I advise you hold it fast in your heart.
Cecilia runs off.

EIGHTH SCENE

Justina, Cyprian, Paracelsus

CYPRIAN Well, I must say, you do make it easy
  For yourself! Magic wands are not at hand,
  It appears, and your craft fails in my house.
PARACELSUS I rather thought it proved itself.
CYPRIAN   Perhaps
  The witchcraft in the market was rehearsed
  With those you so miraculously healed.
  And where Medardus is concerned, I'd guess
  You bought his services cheaply enough.
PARACELSUS Could be.
CYPRIAN   And you call yourself a doctor!
  A tramp is what you are, like those others
  Who succeed at something now and again.
PARACELSUS And consequently unworthy of your
  Continued hospitality. Farewell.
CYPRIAN Oh no! you can't escape so easily.
JUSTINA You see, my husband jests — you're still welcome!
CYPRIAN Of course! As each guest is, in his own way.
  Still, when I've invited one to my house,
  Let him show what he can do. The fiddlers
  I occasionally have in the house,
  They strike up — else I wouldn't let them in.
PARACELSUS It's true. I've yet to earn this cup of wine.

He suddenly steps in front of Justina.

JUSTINA What are you. . .? *She wants to stand up but can't.*

CYPRIAN   Well?

JUSTINA   I want. . .

PARACELSUS   You can't stand up.

CYPRIAN Is it true?

PARACELSUS   Don't be afraid, Justina.
  Your eyes are getting heavy, they are closing.
  You want to open them but can't. You're tired —
  So tired. Sleep is coming, your senses
  Are fading. You are already asleep.
  In an almost conjuring tone
  Quite deep — very deep — you're sleeping. . . dreaming.
  She falls asleep. — Long pause.

CYPRIAN That's excellent. Yes. But now let her dream.

PARACELSUS That I will do. And will, with whispered words,
  Create an entire destiny for her.
  I call it that, you call it a mere dream —
  Will you be content with that?

CYPRIAN   I can't wait.
  Pity that I didn't call the neighbors.
  I could still. . .

PARACELSUS Let it be, they would disturb.
  He bends over Justina.

CYPRIAN What are you doing now? Can't I hear?

PARACELSUS   No.
  I want to see you completely amazed.
  Here, empty this cup — have that much patience.

CYPRIAN But no longer than that!
  *He drinks. Paracelsus whispers something in Justina's ear,
  their positions so that neither his nor her face is visible.*

PARACELSUS *while Cyprian is still drinking.*
                              I'm finished.
CYPRIAN *puts the cup down*   Well?
PARACELSUS Wake up! Justina, wake up!
CYPRIAN   Justina!
PARACELSUS *loudly* Wake up!
  Justina stares at both of them, then at Cyprian, screams and
  runs away into her room, which she bolts from the inside.
CYPRIAN *speechless at first* Justina!
  to Paracelsus   What does this mean? Speak!
  What have you done? . . .
  to the door   Justina!
  to Paracelsus   Does she flee
  From me? What was it you whispered to her?
PARACELSUS Calm down, this is all a game! Moreover,
  She loves you just as much as ever.
CYPRIAN   Why
  Did she run away? And that look! — Justina!
PARACELSUS Stay! She loves you, but remorse torments her.
CYPRIAN Remorse?
PARACELSUS   Yes.
CYPRIAN   Explain yourself, if you please.
PARACELSUS *after a short pause*
  A handsome lad, who left your house just now —
CYPRIAN A handsome. . . who?
PARACELSUS   Named Anselm, I think.
CYPRIAN What of him?
PARACELSUS   The usual thing with squires.
CYPRIAN You mean she's dreaming she loves the squire —?
  A poor jest, truly!
PARACELSUS   How can you think that?
CYPRIAN Well then? Why did she run? Tell me, finally!

PARACELSUS
  Well, because she dreams — what's it concern you?!
CYPRIAN Tell me; I want to know.
PARACELSUS   Very well, then,
  She dreams she once reposed in Anselm's arms.
CYPRIAN She once —
PARACELSUS   Was Anselm's, quite as she is yours.
CYPRIAN You instilled this delusion in her!
PARACELSUS   Yes.
CYPRIAN The jest is — undo it now — *to the door* Justina!
  Very uneasy.
PARACELSUS A dream, friend — what more does it signify?
  You stand for real life — and you know better.
CYPRIAN You could have chosen a different proof
  Of your skill. Look how you've tormented her.
  Release her from this foul dream with all haste.
PARACELSUS Why call it foul? Perhaps she finds it sweet!
CYPRIAN You are without shame! Justina, listen!
  At the door
  She's bolted the door to her room.
PARACELSUS   Farewell!
CYPRIAN You must be out of your mind. Here you stay,
  Damned conjurer, and put an end to this jest!
  It's enough now.
PARACELSUS *vehemently* No, it is not enough!
  You just keep Justina the way she is,
  Guiltless, yet guilty too, since she thinks so.
  Chaste — and yet unchaste, since her memory
  Will now bear images of fiery passion.
  Thus I leave you here with your faithful wife.
CYPRIAN You are mad, and truly will do penance
  For having dared to play so impudent

A trick on me, Master Cyprian.
PARACELSUS   A trick —!?
  Whenever I see anew such a woman,
  Made to bring joy to some exalted man,
  Wasted on such a simpleton as you,
  I grow bitter again! And this one too,
  Among those whom Paracelsus once loved,
  And whom folks — well-advised — handed to you,
  As if a maiden's fate were thus fulfilled —
CYPRIAN Yes, to me; not to a pauper like you!
  Maidens of that kind are for men like me!
PARACELSUS I know they are; I also know one day
  With me would satisfy deeper longings
  Than fifty years spent with a man like you.
CYPRIAN Why are you boasting so? — She's been happy
  As a woman can be, these thirteen years
  Now, at my side.
PARACELSUS   Are you certain of that?
  Because the miserable likes of you
  Have an innate talent to pull such creatures
  Of light down into your circle of dull,
  Wretched comfort — think you, here is her home?
  She's a guest in your house — as much as I.
  I've seen too much loveliness being wasted
  On smug insolence that gives itself airs.
  This is a wrong committed against nature —
  And I try to correct it as I can.
CYPRIAN *furious*
  If you really believe that, wicked man,
  Why do you not force her to go with you,
  Since you have placed her now under your spell —?

PARACELSUS I'm not a thief! You misunderstand me.
  I want to take her from you, not give her
  To another man. Let her remain pure —
  Sullied only for you. With that. . . farewell.
CYPRIAN You will put an end to this sorcery
  Without a moment's delay.
PARACELSUS   No. . . farewell.
CYPRIAN You will stay.
PARACELSUS   Who can command me?
CYPRIAN   I can.
  I'll have you arrested, I'll accuse you
  Of witchcraft.
PARACELSUS Go right ahead. I have time.
CYPRIAN You'll be thrown into the deepest dungeon.
PARACELSUS I'll remain silent, and Justina's dream
  Will last forever.
CYPRIAN   They will torture you.
  They'll kill you.
PARACELSUS Then your last hope that the dream
  Can ever end dies with me, for there is
  No man alive who can free her from it then.
CYPRIAN Lunatic! — Justina, come. . . Justina.
  Don't you hear me?
JUSTINA *from inside* Oh mercy!
CYPRIAN   Open up!
  Justina!
  He draws his sword, smashes the door, pulls Justina out; she
  hides her face.
JUSTINA *sinking to her knees*
          Mercy!
CYPRIAN   Don't be afraid, wife!
JUSTINA I know how good you are!

CYPRIAN   You're innocent.
JUSTINA Don't mock!
CYPRIAN   You're dreaming. You are innocent!
JUSTINA Oh, were it true! I shudder at myself.
  I see myself in his embrace and feel
  His kisses burn my neck, my lips, my cheek —
CYPRIAN It's not true. The sorcerer —
JUSTINA   Yes, you have
  Him to thank for the truth.
CYPRIAN   But it's not true!
  Once more I'm turning to you — yes, I know —
  I have insulted you, you damned scoundrel,
  And do so still — I acknowledge your might,
  You see, I must acknowledge it — but now,
  Be satisfied. Put an end to this torment.
  I'll let you leave freely — nay, more — I'll praise
  Your singular artistry everywhere,
  Only do make my wife wake up at last!
JUSTINA But I am awake. How strangely you speak —
  For heaven's sake, Cyprian! If my guilt
  Clouds your senses — Paracelsus, help him!
CYPRIAN You're begging him to help me —
JUSTINA   Cyprian!
  Forgive me! It's all in the past, you know.
  I will be the best of wives to you now —
  A moment of weakness, that's all it was,
  It will not happen again, rest assured.
  But the moon shone so strangely bright that night.
  Our lilac bushes cast their scent abroad,
  And I was alone in the summer house.
PARACELSUS Go on —
CYPRIAN   Be quiet!

JUSTINA   Let me tell you all,
  And make it good thereby!
CYPRIAN   I'll not listen!
PARACELSUS Let her talk! Who knows what you'll discover!
Cyprian is most perplexed.
JUSTINA I was all alone in the summer house —
  And you — you had gone off to the tavern.
PARACELSUS Have you never done that?
CYPRIAN   What man hasn't?
JUSTINA And then he came — and took me by the hand —
  And kissed me — and spoke such passionate words —
  And then — and then — oh Cyprian, forgive me!
CYPRIAN There's nothing to forgive! You're dreaming!
PARACELSUS   Who knows?
CYPRIAN You do — as well as I!
PARACELSUS   Is she no woman?
  Anselm no man —? Is there no summer house?
CYPRIAN *extremely frightened*
  You're — saying —
PARACELSUS   What if it were just the truth
  That I simply shook awake in her heart?
CYPRIAN You planted this delusion in her mind —
  And now you doubt it yourself?
PARACELSUS   I'm merely
  A sorcerer — Justina is a woman!
CYPRIAN You are driving me crazy —
PARACELSUS   Who can tell
  Whether she dreams what she experienced too?
CYPRIAN You think — she — *He rushes up to her.*
PARACELSUS *to himself*   Is the flood of my own magic
  Closing over my head in scorn? And are
  The boundaries blurring even for me —?

NINTH SCENE

Cyprian, Justina, Paracelsus. Anselm enters.

Justina cries out. Anselm takes fright, looks at everyone. Cyprian and Paracelsus observe him; pause — he starts to go towards Justina.

CYPRIAN *stepping up to Anselm*
  She has confessed —
ANSELM   What?
PARACELSUS   How frightened he gets.
JUSTINA Get out of my sight!
ANSELM   But what have I done?
CYPRIAN She has confessed. Denials are useless.
ANSELM Justina!
JUSTINA   I don't want to see you again.
  Go! You deprived me of my peace of mind,
  Destroyed the joy of our home forever,
  Ruined so much for so fleeting a bliss!
  Oh, how my spirit is consumed by shame
  That I was the victim of your bold youth
  And my unguarded senses. Woe is me,
  That ever I set foot in the summer house!
ANSELM *takes fright*
  For heaven's sake, hush, you're speaking madness!
CYPRIAN *draws his sword*
  Confess!
JUSTINA Confess!
PARACELSUS   Confess!
ANSELM   Confess to what?

CYPRIAN Has your cowardly heart no more boldness
   Than suffices to approach a woman?
ANSELM Justina! . . . This revenge was not noble!
CYPRIAN What? You call it revenge that she repents?
   Wretch!
ANSELM *with noble bearing*
         I'll face your sword at whatever time
   You appoint. But let me declare before
   We fight, my trespass is negligible.
   I did no more than love your beauteous wife.
   And I dared tell her so.
CYPRIAN   Go on — go on!
ANSELM That is all!
JUSTINA   No! No! He wants to spare me . . .
   Won't you understand at last, it's useless
   To deny anything since, in remorse,
   I confessed all to my husband myself.
ANSELM *suddenly, to Paracelsus*
   Damned master wizard, this is your doing!
CYPRIAN Let him be! I have much to thank him for,
   He brought truth into this abode of lies,
   He's my friend, I apologize to him
   For everything before.
PARACELSUS   Go easy now!
   Like a jumble of precious stones, some false,
   Others genuine, that's how the fullness
   Of the past hour lies spread before us here.
   What is to be rejected, what is gain,
   I know that no more now — than you yourselves.
   Truly! More for my own sake than for yours,
   I'll undo the muddle I created.
   Justina! Go to sleep!

ANSELM   Say, where am I?
PARACELSUS *loudly*
  Go to sleep!
CYPRIAN   What do you want?
PARACELSUS   A deep sleep,
  Very deep. . . deeper, yes, — asleep. . . that's good!
  Justina has sunk into the chair, motionless
  Justina, do you hear me?
JUSTINA *sleeping*   I hear you.
PARACELSUS Pay attention! You've forgotten everything,
  From the moment I first put you to sleep
  To when I bid you wake now. This past hour
  I disperse — as if it had never been!
  And now —
CYPRIAN   What now? What good is this to us,
  When she wakes, and finds this hour vanished
  From her memory? What will I know then?
  What if she did speak the truth in her dream!
PARACELSUS I'll see to that. — Pay attention, Justina:
  One thing I command you: when you awake,
  Be truthful, truthful as never before —
  As much, no, more than you were accustomed
  To being with yourself, so that your soul
  Will lie here like a clear stream in sunlight,
  Illuminated to its very bed —
  Until the evening of this fruitful day
  Releases you from this last magic spell.
CYPRIAN   Why until evening only?
PARACELSUS   It's enough.
  You will be glad to see the sun go down, —
  And were she the best of women.
ANSELM   I wait

In vain for an answer to this puzzle.
PARACELSUS Wake up Justina. . . and speak true. Wake up!
JUSTINA *opens her eyes and speaks at once, as if nothing had*
happened.
  Say — how much longer will you stare at me?!
  It's useless! — Your magic isn't working.
  And even if your glance had all the power
  It did when you were still called Hohenheim —
  I mean — for me — that's over! Oh — Anselm?
  How did you get here? I didn't hear you!
  Have you dropped in to say good-bye to us?
ANSELM You know. . . Justina. . .
JUSTINA   It's good you're leaving,
  And I won't rest easy until you're home
  In your father's castle.
ANSELM   You. . . mean —?
JUSTINA   It's time!
  We would have parted less innocently,
  Had you remained here even one more night.
  I still can feel the last stirrings of youth.
  Springtime coaxes, and beauty beckons me.
  Hence I'm glad you're going, and quickly too,
  For where would all this lead to in the end?
  A little bliss, and much fear and remorse.
  I'll be spared all this. As a faithful wife.
  to Cyprian
  If I can continue meeting your glance
  When you watch me, it means you may trust me.
CYPRIAN By God, that I will!
JUSTINA   A peaceable joy,
  For all its lack of fire, is still best.

TENTH SCENE

Cyprian, Justina, Paracelsus, Anselm. Cecilia enters.

ANSELM *very glad at Cecilia's arrival*
  My honored Miss, it gives me great pleasure
  To see you once more; I'm taking my leave —
  I'm leaving Basel today, forever.
CECILIA *smiling*
  So, it is serious.
JUSTINA   You're smiling — that's good.
  A childish dream is fading. You see it
  In me.
CECILIA What is she talking —
JUSTINA   My dear child,
  You'll forget the handsome squire very soon.
ANSELM Cecilia. . . say. . . what's —
PARACELSUS   Listen carefully!
CECILIA Justina. . . Brother!
  Pleading for help.
CYPRIAN   Hush! She sees the light!
JUSTINA You see, *indicating Paracelsus*
                    I truly did love this man once,
  For a long time. . . Oh, Cyprian, how long!
  When you went away, thirteen years ago,
  With no good-bye, or word about returning,
  I thought I'd die. Had you come back again
  On that night you left town — oh, I'd gladly
  Have given you whatever you asked me,
  Even had I known the following day

Would take you from me for good — that's how much
I loved you! Who knows how many windows
In town stand open for one who — never comes!
CYPRIAN What else must I hear! — Oh, let sundown come!
CECILIA Justina!
JUSTINA   Theophrastus, do you recall?
— But see how all things turn out for the best:
Today I thank God you left the city
On that night and lacked sufficient boldness.
What would I be today! — While you conquered
The boundless world, I would have gone to ruin
At home amid shame and scorn. See, Cyprian,
How really close you came to losing me!
And you didn't have a clue — typically.
You thought that once we were safely married,
You could be assured of my tenderness.
Nevertheless — had you felt on some nights
How distant from you I was — you would've been
Much less proud of the woman in your arms!
But presence has power and overcomes
The greatest absent foe with little effort.
And so you won me over, my Cyprian,
And I am yours — and would like to stay so.
CYPRIAN But now the absent foe is here again. . .
JUSTINA Yes — he's here — still, it's not him. . . It's almost
As if something separates me from him
More profoundly than from anyone else.
He stands here now like one who signifies
But does not exist — a ghost from my youth.
And thus, sister, rest assured, will it be
For you concerning our squire Anselm.
You will smile at the folly which today

Seems to be life's purpose —
ANSELM *moved*   Not folly, no —
  I was the fool. . . but I dare not say more —
  This hour strikes me as most marvelous.
  It shimmers and sparkles with vital truth.
  I have an inkling who effected it!
  How he did it — I'm unable to grasp —
  Yet I know, that some understanding stirs
  In me too, and that I did grievous wrong
  In raising my bold eye to this lady.
  In your mercy forgive my youthful pride,
  My noble Master — and give me your hand.
  Things grow gradually more clear — The fog lifts
  And there is much I'm beginning to grasp.
  He looks at Cecilia.

ELEVENTH SCENE

The former, Copus

COPUS *still at the door*
  Greetings to you all. Is the news known yet
  In this noble circle?
CYPRIAN   Permit me, first —
  introducing
  Doctor Copus, our City Physician —
COPUS *bowing*
  Herr Theophrastus Hohenheim —
PARACELSUS   I am.
COPUS Then I may bring the news to you myself,
  Which I meant to tell this noble circle.

I'm just now coming from the City Council.
A motion was introduced and approved,
Of the utmost importance, Sir, for you.
PARACELSUS Banishment?
COPUS   If only it were! Sorry.
PARACELSUS Orders have been issued for my arrest?
COPUS What are you saying?
PARACELSUS *smiling*   The pyre threatens?
COPUS How little you know fair Basel! Listen:
  To pay you homage, the Council wishes
  To create a new honor, and names you
  Second City Physician. I'm the first.
  Are you surprised?
PARACELSUS   I thank the noble Council.
COPUS That means — you accept the post?
PARACELSUS   I cannot.
COPUS Don't say that, Sir. You can! Since I'm the first,
  You'll have solid support in me, my friend.
  I will gladly instruct you in some things.
  In hard cases you can come for advice.
  A Master always welcomes modest students.
PARACELSUS Sorry, I'm scarce suited for such a post,
  Nor would you be satisfied, I'm afraid.
  Here is not my home, I'll be moving on,
  I'm leaving town this very night.
COPUS   You are?
CYPRIAN You're leaving?
PARACELSUS   And bidding you all farewell.
CYPRIAN But please, before you go, explain yourself,
  For else you'll leave us all bewildered here.
  Were you in earnest? Or was it all play?
JUSTINA What are these strange questions?

COPUS   What does he mean?
PARACELSUS It was play! What should it be otherwise?
  What do we do on earth that isn't play,
  May it seem ever so great and profound.
  One man plays with wild mercenary bands,
  Another with mad, superstitious fools.
  Somebody else perhaps with suns or stars.
  I play with human souls. Meaning is found
  Only by him who searches for it.
  Dreaming and waking, truth and lie mingle.
  There's no certainty anywhere. We know
  Nothing of others, nothing of ourselves;
  We always play. Wise is the man who knows it.
  Exits.
JUSTINA *as if waking*
  What happened here? — I think I talked as much
  About myself as I — never intended.
COPUS I don't understand a thing I'm hearing —
  What happened? What was the swindler doing here?
CYPRIAN I don't know if it was meant to do good,
  Yet good it was, therefore let us praise him.
  A whirlwind came, which tore open the gates
  To our souls for a few brief moments,
  And we have cast a fleeting glance inside. . .
  It's over now, the gates are falling shut. —
  Still, what I've seen today shall protect me
  From this time forward from excessive pride.
  It was play, yet I found its meaning out
  And know that I am on the proper path.

                        Curtain

THE GREEN COCKATOO

Grotesque in One Act

CHARACTERS

EMILE, DUKE OF CADIGNAN
FRANÇOIS, VISCOUNT OF NOGEANT
ALBIN, CHEVALIER DE LA TREMOUILLE
THE MARQUIS OF LANSAC
SEVERINE, *his wife*
ROLLIN, *poet*
PROSPERE, *innkeeper, former theater manager*
HENRI
BALTHASAR
GUILLAUME
SCAEVOLA
JULES
ETIENNE
MAURICE
GEORGETTE
MICHETTE
FLIPOTTE
LEOCADIE, *actress, Henri's wife*
GRASSET, *philosopher*
LEBRET, *tailor*
GRAIN, *a hoodlum*
THE POLICE INSPECTOR
NOBLES, ACTORS, ACTRESSES, CITIZENS

The action takes place in Paris, on the evening of July 14, 1789, in "The Green Cockatoo," Prospère's subterranean tavern.

> *The Inn "The Green Cockatoo"*
> *A not very large room, below street level, accessible by seven*
> *steps located fairly far back on the right. A door at the top of the*
> *stairs. A second door, barely visible, is in the background, left.*
> *A number of plain wooden tables and chairs almost fill the entire*
> *room. In the middle, towards the left, the bar; behind it, a*
> *number of barrels with taps. The room is lit by oil lamps which*
> *are hanging down from the ceiling.*

The INNKEEPER PROSPERE; *the citizens* LEBRET *and*
GRASSET *enter.*

GRASSET *still on the steps* In here, Lebrêt; I know my
sources. My old friend and manager always has a barrel of
wine stashed away somewhere, even if all Paris is dying of
thirst.

PROSPERE Good evening, Grasset. So, you're back again? All
done with philosophy? Want me to hire you again?

GRASSET Yeah, sure! Wine is what I want from you. I'm the
guest — you're the innkeeper.

PROSPERE Wine? Where am I supposed to get wine, Grasset?
You know they looted all the wine shops in Paris last night.
And I'll bet you were in on it.

GRASSET Let's have the wine. As for that rabble that'll be
here in an hour. . . . *Listening* You hear anything, Lebrêt?

LEBRET It sounds like faraway thunder.

GRASSET Gallant — citizens of Paris. . . . *To Prospère* For
that rabble you still have a supply, I'm sure. So, let's have it.
My friend and admirer, Citizen Lebrêt, tailor in the Rue St.
Honoré, will pay for everything.

LEBRET Certainly, certainly, I'll pay for everything.

PROSPERE *hesitates.*

GRASSET Go on, Lebrêt, show him you have money.

LEBRET *pulls out his purse.*

PROSPERE Well, I'll see whether I. . . . *He opens the tap of one of the barrels and fills two glasses.* Where are you coming from, Grasset? From the Palais Royal?

GRASSET That's right. . . I gave a speech there. Yes indeed, my friend, now it's my turn. Do you know whom I spoke after?

PROSPERE Well?

GRASSET After Camille Desmoulins! Yes indeed, I dared to do it. And tell me, Lebrêt, who got the greater applause, Desmoulins or me?

LEBRET You . . . without a doubt.

GRASSET And how did I look?

LEBRET Magnificent.

GRASSET Hear that, Prospère? I stood up on a table. . . I looked like a statue. . . that's right — and all the thousand, five thousand, ten thousand gathered around me — exactly as they had around Camille Desmoulins earlier. . . and cheered me on.

LEBRET It was a louder cheer.

GRASSET That's right. . . not by much, but it was louder. And now they're all headed for the Bastille. . . and I may say, they heeded my call. I swear to you, before the night is over we'll have 'em.

PROSPERE Yes, of course, if the walls collapse from all your speeches.

GRASSET What do you mean — speeches! Are you deaf? Our gallant soldiers are there. They feel the same infernal fury towards that damned prison as we do. They know that behind those walls their brothers and fathers lie captive. . . . But they wouldn't shoot if we hadn't spoken. My dear Prospère,

the power of the intellect is great. Here — *to Lebrêt* Where
do you have the papers?

LEBRET Here. . . . *pulls some pamphlets out of his pocket.*

GRASSET Here are the latest pamphlets that were just distribut-
ed at the Palais Royal. Here's one by my friend Cerutti, "A
Memorial for the French People," here's one by Desmoulins
who, of course, speaks better than he writes. . . "Free
France."

PROSPERE When will yours finally appear, the one you're
always talking about?

GRASSET We don't need any more. The time has come for
action. He's a knave who keeps within his four walls today.
Whoso would be a man must go out into the streets!

LEBRET Bravo, bravo!

GRASSET In Toulon they killed the mayor, in Brignolles they
looted a dozen houses. . . only we in Paris are still such
dullards as to put up with everything.

PROSPERE One really cannot say that any longer.

LEBRET *who has been drinking all along* Arise, ye citizens,
arise!

GRASSET Arise!. . . Lock up this dive of yours and come with
us now!

PROSPERE I'll come all right, when it's time.

GRASSET Yeah, sure, when there's no more danger.

PROSPERE My friend, I love freedom as much as you — but
my profession comes first.

GRASSET There's only one profession for the citizens of Paris
now: the liberation of their brothers.

PROSPERE Yes, for those who have nothing else to do!

LEBRET What's he saying there! . . . He's mocking us!

PROSPERE Wouldn't dream of it. — Better see to it that you get out of here. . . my show is starting soon. I have no use for you in that.

LEBRET What kind of show? . . . Is this a theater?

PROSPERE Certainly it's a theater. Your friend was still playing here two weeks ago.

LEBRET You played here, Grasset? . . . Why do you let this guy mock you without saying a word?

GRASSET Calm down. . . yes, it's true; I played here, since it's no ordinary tavern. . . it's a refuge for criminals. . . come along. . . .

PROSPERE First you'll pay.

LEBRET If this is a refuge for criminals then I won't pay a sou.

PROSPERE Explain to your friend where he is, will you.

GRASSET It's a strange place! People come here who play criminals — and others who are criminals without suspecting it.

LEBRET Is that so —?

GRASSET I call to your attention that what I just said is very witty; it could form the basis of an entire speech.

LEBRET I don't understand a thing you're saying.

GRASSET But I told you that Prospère was my manager. And he's still putting on shows with his people; only in a different way than before. My former colleagues sit around here and act as if they were criminals. You understand? They tell hair-raising stories about events they've never experienced — speak of crimes they've never committed. . . and the audience that comes here has the pleasant thrill of sitting among the most dangerous rabble in Paris — among swindlers, burglars, murderers — and —

LEBRET What kind of audience?

PROSPERE The most fashionable people in Paris.

GRASSET Nobles. . . .

PROSPERE Gentlemen from court —

LEBRET Down with them!

GRASSET It's just the thing for them. It shakes their jaded senses up for them. Here I began, Lebrêt, here I made my first speech, as if it were in jest. . . and here I started to hate the dogs who sat among us in their beautiful clothes, perfumed, gorged full. . . and I'm very pleased, my dear Lebrêt, that you're getting the chance to see the place where your great friend began. *In a different tone* Say, Prospère, supposing this business were to go wrong. . . .

PROSPERE What business?

GRASSET Well, the business with my political career. . . would you take me on again?

PROSPERE Not for all the world!

GRASSET *lightly* Why not? — Maybe someone else could come into fashion besides your Henri.

PROSPERE Leaving that aside. . . I'd be afraid you might forget yourself some time — and attack one of my paying guests in earnest.

GRASSET *flattered* That would be possible, certainly.

PROSPERE I, on the other hand. . . I keep myself under control.

GRASSET Frankly, Prospère, I have to tell you that I would admire you for your self-control if I didn't happen to know you're a coward.

PROSPERE Ah, my friend, it's enough for me that I can accomplish something in my own line. It gives me sufficient pleasure to be able to tell these fellows my opinion to their faces and to insult them to my heart's content — while they think it's all in jest. It's also a way of getting rid of one's rage. — *Pulls out a dagger and lets it flash.*

LEBRET Citizen Prospère, what's the meaning of this?

GRASSET Don't be afraid. I'll bet the dagger hasn't even been sharpened.

PROSPERE You may be wrong there, my friend; sometime or other the day will come when the joke turns to earnest — and for that I am prepared in any case.

GRASSET The day is near. We live in a great time! Come, Citizen Lebrêt, let's join our comrades. Prospère, farewell, you'll next see me as a great man, or never again.

LEBRET *reeling* As a great man. . . or. . . never again. — *They exit.*

PROSPERE *remains, sits down at a table, opens one of the pamphlets and reads aloud to himself* "Now the beast has its head in the noose, throttle it!" — He doesn't write badly, the little Desmoulins. "Never has a richer booty offered itself to the victors. Forty thousand palaces and castles, two-fifths of all the property in France will be the reward for bravery, — those who think themselves conquerors will be subdued, the nation will be purged."

INSPECTOR *enters.*

PROSPERE *sizes him up* Well, the rabble showing up early today?

INSPECTOR My dear Prospère, don't joke with me; I'm the Police Inspector for your district.

PROSPERE And how may I be of service?

INSPECTOR I've been ordered to attend your show this evening.

PROSPERE It will be a special honor for me.

INSPECTOR That's not the reason, my dearest Prospère. The authorities want to be clear as to what actually goes on in this place. For several weeks —

PROSPERE It's a place of amusement, Inspector, nothing more.

INSPECTOR Let me finish. For several weeks now, this establishment has been said to be the scene of wild orgies.

PROSPERE You've been falsely informed, Inspector. We make jokes here, nothing more.

INSPECTOR That's how it starts. I know. But it ends up otherwise, according to my information. You were an actor?

PROSPERE Manager, Inspector. Manager of an excellent company which last performed in Denis.

INSPECTOR That's irrelevant. Then you came into a small inheritance?

PROSPERE Not worth talking about, Inspector.

INSPECTOR Your company disbanded?

PROSPERE My inheritance no less.

INSPECTOR *smiling* Pretty good. *Both smile. — Suddenly serious* You started a tavern?

PROSPERE Which went miserably.

INSPECTOR — Whereupon you hit on an idea which, one cannot deny, has a certain originality.

PROSPERE You flatter me, Inspector.

INSPECTOR You reassembled your company and allow them to play a strange and not entirely unobjectionable comedy here.

PROSPERE If it were objectionable, Inspector, then I wouldn't have my audience — I can say, the most elegant audience in Paris. The Viscount of Nogeant is my guest daily. The Marquis of Lansac comes quite often; and the Duke of Cadignan, Inspector, is the most enthusiastic admirer of my leading actor, the famous Henri Baston.

INSPECTOR As well as of the art, or artistry of your female artistes, I imagine.

PROSPERE If you knew my artistes, Inspector, you wouldn't hold that against anyone in the world.

INSPECTOR Enough. It has been reported to the authorities that the entertainment which your — how shall I say —

PROSPERE The word "artists" ought to suffice.

INSPECTOR I think I'll settle on the word "accomplices" — that the entertainment which your "accomplices" offer exceeds in every sense what is permissible. We've heard there are speeches given here by — how shall I say — by your artistic criminals — which — just how does my report put it? *He reads, as he has already done before, from a small notebook* — are likely to have not only an immoral effect, which would trouble us little, but also a highly inflammatory one — which absolutely cannot be a matter of indifference to the authorities in so excitable a time as the one in which we are living.

PROSPERE Inspector, I can only respond to this accusation with the courteous invitation that you see the thing yourself one time. You will notice that nothing inflammatory at all happens here, if only for the reason that my audience does not allow itself to be inflamed. What takes place here is a theatrical performance — that's all.

INSPECTOR Naturally, I do not accept your invitation; nevertheless, I will stay here by virtue of my office.

PROSPERE I believe I can promise you the best entertainment, Inspector; but permit me to suggest that you take off your uniform and appear in civilian clothes. You see, if a police inspector in uniform were to be seen here, the spontaneity of my artists as well as the mood of my audience would suffer.

INSPECTOR You are right; I'll go and return as an elegant young man.

PROSPERE That will be easy for you, Inspector; you'll be welcome as a scoundrel too — that wouldn't attract attention — only not as an inspector.

INSPECTOR Good-bye. *Moves towards the exit.*

PROSPERE *bows* When will that blessed day come when you and your ilk. . . .

INSPECTOR *at the door, runs into Grain, who is extremely ragged and who starts when he sees the Inspector. The latter sizes him up at first, then smiles, and turns obligingly to Prospère* One of your artists already? . . . *Exits.*

GRAIN *speaks tearfully, pathetically* Good evening.

PROSPERE *after looking at him a long while* If you're one of my company, I won't deny you my appreciation, because I do not recognize you.

GRAIN What do you mean?

PROSPERE So, no kidding, take the wig off, I do want to know who you are. *He pulls his hair.*

GRASSET Ow!

PROSPERE But this is real — Damn. . . who are you? . . . You seem to be a real tramp.

GRAIN That's right.

PROSPERE What is it you want from me?

GRAIN Have I the honor of speaking to Citizen Prospère. . . Innkeeper of "The Green Cockatoo"?

PROSPERE That's me.

GRAIN I call myself Grain. . . sometimes Carniche. . . on some occasions the Screaming Pumice — but under the name Grain I was locked up, Citizen Prospère — and that's the relevant point.

PROSPERE Ah — I understand. You want to get a job here and are playing a bit for me right off. That's good too. Go on.

GRAIN Citizen Prospère, don't mistake me for a swindler. I'm a man of honor. If I say I was locked up then it's the entire truth.

Prospère looks at him distrustfully.

GRAIN *pulls a piece of paper from his jacket* Here, Citizen Prospère. You'll see from this that I was released yesterday afternoon at four.

PROSPERE After serving two years — damn, this is genuine!

GRAIN Did you really doubt it, Citizen Prospère?

PROSPERE But what did you do that they locked you up for two years —?

GRAIN They would've hanged me; but fortunately for me I was still half a child when I killed my poor aunt.

PROSPERE Man alive, how can one kill his own aunt?

GRAIN Citizen Prospère, I wouldn't have done it if my aunt hadn't deceived me with my best friend.

PROSPERE Your aunt?

GRAIN That's right — she was closer to me than aunts usually are to their nephews. They were — unusual family relationships. . . I was bitter, extremely bitter. May I tell you about it?

PROSPERE Go right ahead, perhaps we'll be able to do business.

GRAIN My sister was still half a child when she ran away from home — and what do you think — with whom? —

PROSPERE It's difficult to guess.

GRAIN With my uncle! And he abandoned her — with a child.

PROSPERE With a whole one — I hope.

GRAIN It is indelicate of you, Citizen Prospère, to joke about such things.

PROSPERE I'm going to tell you something, you Screaming Pumice. Your family history bores me. Do you think I'm here to let every tramp who comes running in tell me who he murdered? What do I care about that? I assume you want something from me —

GRAIN Yes I do, Citizen Prospère, I've come to ask you for work.

PROSPERE *scornfully* Let me call to your attention that there are no aunts to murder here; this is an entertainment establishment.

GRAIN Oh, I had enough with that one time. I want to become a respectable human being — I was told to look you up.

PROSPERE By whom, if I may ask?

GRAIN An amiable young man they locked in my cell three days ago. Now he's alone. His name is Gaston. . . and you know him. —

PROSPERE Gaston! Now I know why he's been missing these past three evenings. One of my best portrayers of pickpockets. — He told stories; — ah, the people shivered.

GRAIN Yes. And now they've nabbed him!

PROSPERE What do you mean nabbed? He didn't really steal.

GRAIN He did. But it must've been his first time, since he seems to have gone about it with incredible clumsiness. Imagine — *confidentially* — on the Boulevard des Capucines, simply reached into a lady's pocketbook — and pulled out her purse — an absolute amateur. — You inspire confidence in me, Citizen Prospère — and so I'll confess to you — there was a time when I pulled off similar little tricks, but never without my dear father. When I was still a child, when we all still lived together, when my poor aunt was still alive —

PROSPERE What are you whining about? I find that in bad taste! You shouldn't have killed her!

GRAIN Too late. But what I was driving at — take me in here. I want to go in the opposite direction from Gaston. He played a criminal and became one — I. . . .

PROSPERE I'll give you a try. Your disguise will have an effect, all right. And at an opportune moment you'll simply tell about the business with your aunt. The way it was. Someone will ask you, I'm sure.

GRAIN I thank you, Citizen Prospère. And as far as my salary is concerned —

PROSPERE Today you're auditioning for the job, so I can't pay you any salary yet. — You'll get plenty to eat and drink. . . and a couple of francs for a place to sleep won't be of much consequence either.

GRAIN I thank you. And simply introduce me to your other members as a guest from the provinces.

PROSPERE Oh no. . . we'll tell them right away that you're a real murderer. They'll like that much better.

GRAIN I'm sorry, I certainly don't want to create any trouble for myself — but this I don't understand.

PROSPERE Once you've been in the theater for any length of time you'll understand it all right.

SCAEVOLA *and* JULES *enter.*

SCAEVOLA Good evening, boss!

PROSPERE Innkeeper. . . . How many more times do I have to tell you, the entire joke goes to the dogs if you call me "boss."

SCAEVOLA Whatever you are, I don't think we'll be playing tonight.

PROSPERE Why's that?

SCAEVOLA The people won't be in the mood —. There's a hell of a racket in the streets, and in front of the Bastille especially they're screaming like they were possessed.

PROSPERE What business is that of ours? That screaming has been going for months and our audience hasn't stayed away. They amuse themselves just as they did before.

SCAEVOLA Yes, they have all the merriment of people who're going to be hanged soon.

PROSPERE If only I live to see it!

SCAEVOLA For the time being, give us something to drink, so I'll get into the right frame of mind. I am not at all in the right frame of mind today.

PROSPERE That happens to you quite often, my friend. I have to tell you, I was thoroughly dissatisfied with you yesterday.

SCAEVOLA How so, if I may ask?

PROSPERE That story about the burglary you graced us with was simply silly.

SCAEVOLA Silly?

PROSPERE That's right. Completely unbelievable. Bellowing alone won't do it.

SCAEVOLA I did not bellow.

PROSPERE Go on, you bellow all the time. It's really becoming necessary for me to rehearse the bits with all of you. I can't rely on your own ideas. Henri is the only one.

SCAEVOLA Henri, always Henri. Henri is a ham. That burglary yesterday was a masterpiece. Henri couldn't bring something like that off as long as he lives. — If I'm not good enough for you, my friend, then I'll simply go to a regular theater. This here's just a bunch of vagabonds anyway. . . .

Ah. . . . *notices Grain* Who is this? . . . He isn't one of us?
Have you hired a new man, maybe? What sort of disguise
does the fellow have?

PROSPERE Calm down, he's not a professional actor. He's a
real murderer.

SCAEVOLA Oh, I see. . . *goes up to him* Very pleased to
meet you. Scaevola is my name.

GRAIN I'm called Grain.

*Jules has been walking about the room the entire time,
sometimes coming to a stop as well, like one inwardly
tortured.*

PROSPERE What's the matter with you, Jules?

JULES I'm rehearsing.

PROSPERE What?

JULES Pangs of conscience. I'm doing a man with pangs of
conscience tonight. What do you say to the furrow here, on
my forehead? Don't I look as if all the furies of hell. . . .
paces back and forth.

SCAEVOLA *bellows* Wine — wine here!

PROSPERE Calm down. . . there's no audience yet, you know.

HENRI *and* LEOCADIE *enter.*

HENRI Good evening! *He greets those sitting at the back with
a casual wave* Good evening, gentlemen!

PROSPERE Good evening, Henri! What's this I see! With
Léocadie!

GRAIN *has looked at Léocadie attentively; to Scaevola* Why,
I know her. . . . *Speaks softly with the others.*

LEOCADIE Yes, my dear Prospère, it's me!

PROSPERE I haven't seen you for a whole year. Let me say
hello to you. *He moves to kiss her.*

HENRI Stop that! — *His glance frequently comes to rest on Léocadie with pride and passion, but also with a certain fear.*

PROSPERE But Henri. . . old colleagues! . . . Your former boss, Léocadie!

LEOCADIE Where has the time gone, Prospère! . . .

PROSPERE What are you sighing about? If anyone has made a career of it, then it's you! Of course, a beautiful young woman always has it easier than we do.

HENRI *furious* Stop that.

PROSPERE Why do you keep yelling at me like that? Because you're back together with her again?

HENRI Be quiet! — Since yesterday she's my wife.

PROSPERE Your. . . ? *To Léocadie* Is he kidding?

LEOCADIE He really married me. Yes. —

PROSPERE Then I congratulate you. Well. . . Scaevola, Jules — Henri has gotten married.

SCAEVOLA *comes forward* My best wishes! *Winks at Léocadie.*

JULES *shakes hands with both of them.*

GRAIN *to Prospère* How odd — I've seen this woman . . . a few minutes after I was set free again.

PROSPERE What do you mean?

GRAIN She was the first pretty woman I saw after two years. I was very moved. But it was a different gentlemen with whom — *continues to speak to Prospère.*

HENRI *in an exalted tone, as if inspired, but not declamatory* Léocadie, my love, my wife! . . . Everything in the past is over now. Much is blotted out at a moment like this.

Scaevola and Jules have gone to the rear, Prospère comes forward again.

PROSPERE What sort of moment?

HENRI Now we are united by a holy sacrament. This is more than human oaths. Now God is watching over us, we can forget everything that happened before. Léocadie, a new day is dawning. Léocadie, everything's becoming sacred, our kisses, be they ever so wild, will be sacred from now on. Léocadie, my love, my wife! . . . *He looks at her with glowing eyes.* Say, doesn't she look different than before, Prospère? Is her forehead not pure? What was is blotted out. Isn't that right, Léocadie?

LEOCADIE Certainly, Henri.

HENRI And everything's fine. Tomorrow we're leaving Paris, Léocadie is appearing tonight for the last time at the Porte St. Martin, and I'm playing here for the last time tonight.

PROSPERE *perplexed* Are you out of your senses, Henri? — You want to leave me? And the manager at the Porte St. Martin wouldn't dream of letting Léocadie go, would he? She's the secret of the success of his place. I've heard the young gentlemen are pouring in.

HENRI Be quiet. Léocadie will go with me. She will never leave me. Tell me you will never leave me, Léocadie. *Brutally* Tell me!

LEOCADIE I will never leave you!

HENRI If you did, I would. . . . *Pause* I'm fed up with this life. I want peace, peace is what I want.

PROSPERE But what do you intend to do, Henri? This is ridiculous. I'll make you a proposition. You can take Léocadie away from the Porte St. Martin for all I care — but let her stay here, with me. I'll hire her. I'm short of talented female performers anyhow.

HENRI I have made my decision, Prospère. We're leaving the city. We're moving to the country.

PROSPERE To the country? But where?

HENRI To my old father, who's living all by himself in our poor village, — whom I haven't seen in seven years. He hardly hoped to ever see his lost son again. He'll be glad to take me in.

PROSPERE What do you intend to do in the country? They're starving in the country. People there are doing a thousand times worse than in the city. What will you do there? You're not the man to till the fields. Don't imagine you are.

HENRI I'll turn out to be the man for that too.

PROSPERE Soon there won't be any grain growing anywhere in France. You're heading into certain misery.

HENRI Into happiness, Prospère. Isn't that so, Léocadie? We've often dreamt of it. I long for the peace of the wide plains. Yes, Prospère, in my dreams I see myself walking across the fields with her in the evening, in an endless stillness, the wonderful, comforting sky over us. Yes, we are running away from this terrible and dangerous city, and a great peacefulness will come over us. Isn't that so, Léocadie, we've often dreamt of it?

LEOCADIE Yes, we've often dreamt of it.

PROSPERE Listen, Henri, you should think it over. I'll be glad to raise your salary, and I'll give Léocadie as much as you.

LEOCADIE You hear that, Henri?

PROSPERE I really don't know who's supposed to replace you here. None of my people has such fabulous ideas as you, none is as beloved by the audience as you. . . . Don't leave!

HENRI I can well believe that no one'll replace me.

PROSPERE Stay with me, Henri! *Throws a glance at Léocadie; she indicates that she'll manage it.*

HENRI And I promise you, the farewell will go hard for them — for them, not me. For tonight — for my final appearance, I've prepared something that'll make them all shudder. . . a hint of the end of their world will blow upon them. . . for the end of their world is near. But I will only experience it from far away. . . we'll hear about it, Léocadie, many days after it happens. . . . But they will shudder, I tell you. And you yourself'll say, Henri never played so well.

PROSPERE What will you play? What? Do you know, Léocadie?

LEOCADIE I never know anything.

HENRI Does anyone have any inkling what an artist lies hidden in me?

PROSPERE Certainly we have an inkling, that is why I am telling you that someone with that kind of talent doesn't bury himself in the country. What an injustice to yourself! To art!

HENRI I don't give a damn about art. I want peace. You don't understand that, Prospère, you've never been in love.

PROSPERE Oh! —

HENRI As I am in love. — I want to be alone with her — that's it. . . Léocadie, only that way can we forget everything. But then we're going to be so happy, as no human beings have ever been. We'll have children, you'll be a good mother, Léocadie, and an honest woman. Everything, everything will be blotted out. *Long pause.*

LEOCADIE It's getting late, Henri, I have to get to the theater. Good-bye, Prospère, I'm glad to have had the chance, finally, to see your famous place, where Henri celebrates such triumphs.

PROSPERE Why didn't you ever come here, then?

LEOCADIE Henri didn't want me to — well, you know, on account of all the young people with whom I'd have to sit here.

HENRI *has gone to the rear* Give me a swig, Scaevola. *He drinks.*

PROSPERE *to Léocadie, since Henri can't hear him* A proper
  fool, your Henri — if all you had done is just sit with them.
LEOCADIE Hey, I don't have to take remarks like that.
PROSPERE Take my advice, be careful, you dumb bunny.
  He's going to kill you one day.
LEOCADIE What is it?
PROSPERE Only yesterday you were seen with one of your
  boyfriends again.
LEOCADIE That was no boyfriend you fool, that was. . . .
HENRI *turns around quickly* What's with you two? No jokes,
  if you please. No more whispering. There are no more
  secrets. She is my wife.
PROSPERE What did you give her for a wedding present?
LEOCADIE Oh God, he doesn't think of things like that.
HENRI Well now, you shall have it before the day is over.
LEOCADIE What?
SCAEVOLA, JULES What are you giving her?
HENRI *quite serious* When you're done with your scene you
  may come here and see me perform. *The others laugh.*
  Never has a woman received a more magnificent wedding
  gift. Come, Léocadie; see you later, Prospère, I'll be back
  soon.
  Henri and Léocadie exit. — Entering at the same time are:

FRANÇOIS, VISCOUNT OF NOGEANT, ALBIN, CHEVA-
LIER DE LA TREMOUILLE.

SCAEVOLA What a pitiful braggart.
PROSPERE Good evening, you pigs.
  Albin starts.
FRANÇOIS *without reacting* Wasn't that the little Léocadie
  from the Porte St. Martin who just left with Henri?

PROSPERE Of course it was. How about that? — When all's said and done she could remind even you that you're still something like a man, if she tried really hard.

FRANÇOIS *laughing* It's not out of the question. We've come a bit early tonight, it seems.

PROSPERE In the meantime you can amuse yourself with your little lover boy.

Albin wants to run at him.

FRANÇOIS Stop it. I told you how things work here. Bring us wine.

PROSPERE Yes, that I will. The time will soon come when all of you will be very satisfied with water from the Seine.

FRANÇOIS Sure, sure. . . but for today I'll ask for wine, and the best you have at that.

Prospère goes to the bar.

ALBIN That's one horrible fellow.

FRANÇOIS Just remember, everything is in jest. And besides, there are places where you can get to hear very similar things said in earnest.

ALBIN Isn't it forbidden, then?

FRANÇOIS *laughs* One can tell you're from the provinces.

ALBIN Oh, we have some nice things going on too, these days. The peasants are becoming insolent in a way. . . one hardly knows what to do any more.

FRANÇOIS What do you expect? The poor devils are hungry; that's the secret.

ALBIN What can I do about that? What can my great-uncle do about that?

FRANÇOIS How does your great-uncle come into it?

ALBIN Well, he comes into it because they actually held a meeting in our village — quite openly — and there they simply called my great-uncle, the Count of Tremouille, a grain-profiteer.

FRANÇOIS That's all. . . ?

ALBIN Well, I ask you!

FRANÇOIS We'll go to the Palais Royal tomorrow; there you'll hear the vicious speeches these fellows make. But we let them talk; it's the best thing one can do; basically they're good people, we have to allow them to let off steam this way.

ALBIN *pointing to Scaevola, etc.* What kind of suspicious looking characters are those? Just take a look how they're glaring at us. *He reaches for his sword.*

FRANÇOIS *pulls his hand away.* Don't make yourself ridiculous! *To the three* You needn't begin yet, wait till there's a bigger audience. *To Albin* They are the most respectable people on earth, actors are. I guarantee you, you've sat at the same table with worse swindlers already.

ALBIN But they were dressed better.

Prospère brings wine.

MICHETTE *and* FLIPOTTE *enter.*

FRANÇOIS Hello, kids. Come, sit down here with us.

MICHETTE Here we are. Come on, Flipotte. She's still a bit shy.

FLIPOTTE Good evening, young gentleman!

ALBIN Good evening, ladies!

MICHETTE The little one is cute. *She sits on Albin's lap.*

ALBIN So, please, explain to me, François, are these respectable women?

MICHETTE What's he saying?

FRANÇOIS No, it's not like that; the ladies who come here — God, are you silly, Albin!

PROSPERE What may I bring Your Graces?

MICHETTE Bring a very sweet wine.

FRANÇOIS *indicating Flipotte* A friend?

MICHETTE We live together. In fact, we have only one bed between us!

FLIPOTTE *blushing* Will that be very awkward for you when you come see her? *Sits down on François's lap.*

ALBIN But she isn't shy at all.

SCAEVOLA *stands up, gloomily goes over to the young people's table* So I've found you again at last! *To Albin* And you, you miserable seducer, see to it that you. . . . She's mine!

Prospère watches.

FRANÇOIS *to Albin* A joke, a joke. . . .

ALBIN She is not his —?

MICHETTE Go on, let me sit where I like.

Scaevola stands there with clenched fists.

PROSPERE *behind him* Now, now!

SCAEVOLA Ha, ha!

PROSPERE *grabs him by the collar* Ha, ha! *Aside to him* You can't think of anything else! You haven't got a dime's worth of talent. Bellowing. That's the only thing you know how to do.

MICHETTE *to François* He did it better the other day —

SCAEVOLA *to Prospère* I'm not in the right frame of mind yet. I'll do it again later, when there are more people here; you'll see, Prospère; I need an audience.

THE DUKE OF CADIGNAN *enters.*

DUKE In full swing already!

Michette and Flipotte go over to him.

MICHETTE My sweet Duke!

FRANÇOIS Good evening, Emile! . . . *Introducing* My young friend Albin, Chevalier of Tremouille — the Duke of Cadignan.

DUKE I'm very happy to make your acquaintance. *To the young women, who are clinging to him* Let me go, kids! — *To Albin* So, you're having a look at this strange tavern too?

ALBIN I find it extremely confusing.

FRANÇOIS The Chevalier arrived in Paris only a few days ago.

DUKE *laughing* You've picked a fine time.

ALBIN How so?

MICHETTE My, the perfume he has on again! There isn't another man in Paris with such a pleasant smell. *To Albin* . . . You can't tell that way.

DUKE She's only talking about the seven or eight hundred men she knows as well as me.

FLIPOTTE Will you let me play with your sword? — *She pulls the sword from its scabbard and lets it flash in the light.*

GRAIN *to Prospère* It's him! . . . He's the one I saw her with! — *Prospère lets him tell the story; he seems astonished.*

DUKE Henri isn't here yet? *To Albin* Once you've seen him you won't regret having come here.

PROSPERE *to the Duke* Well, so you're here again too? I'm glad. After all, we won't have the pleasure much longer.

DUKE Why not? I like your place very much.

PROSPERE That I believe. But since you're going to be one of the first in any event. . . .

ALBIN What does that mean?

PROSPERE You understand me well enough. — The very lucky ones will go first! . . . *Goes towards the back.*

DUKE *after pondering briefly* If I were king I'd make him my court jester; I mean, I would keep many court jesters, but he'd be one of them.

ALBIN How did he mean that, that you're too lucky?

DUKE He means, Chevalier. . . .

ALBIN Please, don't call me Chevalier. Everyone calls me Albin, simply Albin, because I look so young.

DUKE *smiling* Fine. . . but then you must call me Emile, all right?

ALBIN If you'll permit me, gladly, Emile.

DUKE They're getting eerie with their jokes, these people.

FRANÇOIS Why eerie? It makes me feel a lot easier. As long as the rabble is disposed to make jokes it won't come to anything serious.

DUKE Except that the jokes are getting to be all too strange. And then I found out something again today that's food for thought.

FRANÇOIS Tell us.

FLIPOTTE, MICHETTE Yes, tell us, sweet Duke!

DUKE Do you know Lelange?

FRANÇOIS Of course — the village. . . the Marquis of Mont-ferrat has one of his most beautiful hunting lodges there.

DUKE Quite right; my brother is at the castle with him now, and he just wrote me about this business I'm going to tell you about. They have a mayor in Lelange who's very unpopular.

FRANÇOIS If you could name me one who is popular —

DUKE Just listen. — Now, the women of the village marched past the mayor's house — with a coffin. . . .

FLIPOTTE What? . . . They carried it? Carried a coffin? I wouldn't want to carry a coffin for all the world.

FRANÇOIS Hush –– no one is asking you to carry a coffin. *To the Duke* Well?

DUKE And a couple of the women went to the mayor's house afterwards and explained to him that he'd have to die — but they would do him the honor of burying him. —

FRANÇOIS Well, did they kill him?

DUKE No — at least my brother doesn't write anything about it.

FRANÇOIS Well then! . . . Brawlers, prattlers, clowns — that's what they are. In Paris today, they're bawling at the Bastille for a change — as they've done half a dozen times already —

DUKE Well — if I were the King, I'd have put an end to it — long ago. . . .

ALBIN Is it true that the King is so kindly?

DUKE You haven't been presented to His Majesty yet?

FRANÇOIS The Chevalier is in Paris for the first time.

DUKE Yes, you are incredibly young. How old, if one may ask?

ALBIN I only look so young, I'm already seventeen. . . .

DUKE Seventeen — how much still lies before you. I'm twenty-four already. . . I'm beginning to regret how much of my youth I've missed.

FRANÇOIS *laughs* That's a good one! You, Duke. . . for whom every day is wasted in which you haven't conquered a woman or stabbed a man to death.

DUKE The only misfortune is that one almost never conquers the right woman — and always runs the wrong man through. And thus one's youth slips away after all. It is quite as Rollin says.

FRANÇOIS What does Rollin say?

DUKE I was thinking of his new play that they're playing at the Comédie — there's such a pretty simile in it. Don't you remember?

FRANÇOIS I have no mind at all for verses —

DUKE I don't either, unfortunately. . . I remember only the sense. . . . He says that youth which one fails to enjoy is like a shuttlecock left lying in the sand instead of being tossed in the air.

ALBIN *precociously* I find that entirely accurate.

DUKE Isn't it? — The feathers do gradually lose their color and fall out. Better for it to fall in some bushes where it is never found again.

ALBIN How are we to understand that, Emile?

DUKE It's more a matter of feeling it. If I knew the lines you'd understand it right away.

ALBIN It appears to me, Emile, that you could write verses too if only you wanted to.

DUKE Why?

ALBIN It seems to me that this place has come to life since you've been here —

DUKE *smiling* Really? Has it come to life?

FRANÇOIS Won't you sit down with us?

Two noblemen enter in the meantime and sit down at a somewhat distant table; Prospère appears to be insulting them.

DUKE I can't stay. But I'll come back again in any case.

MICHETTE Stay with me!

FLIPOTTE Take me with you!

They try to hold him back.

PROSPERE *coming forward* Just leave him alone! You're not bad enough for him, not by a long shot. He has to run to a streetwalker, that's where he feels best.

DUKE I'll be back for sure, if only not to miss Henri.

FRANÇOIS Imagine, Henri was just leaving with Léocadie as we came in.

DUKE So. — He married her. Did you know that?

FRANÇOIS Really? — What will the others say to that?

ALBIN What others?

FRANÇOIS She is universally loved, you know.

DUKE And he wants to go away with her. . . what do I know
. . . somebody told me.

PROSPERE Is that so? Somebody told you? — *Looks at the
Duke.*

DUKE *looks at Prospère, then* It's too silly. Léocadie was
created to be the greatest, the most magnificent courtesan in
the world.

FRANÇOIS Who doesn't know that?

DUKE Is there anything more imprudent than taking people
away from their true profession? *Since François laughs* I
don't mean that as a joke. One has to be born to be a courtesan too — the same as a conqueror or an author.

FRANÇOIS You are paradoxical.

DUKE I feel sorry for her — and for Henri. He ought to stay
here — no, not here — I'd like to get him into the Comédie
— although even there — I always feel as if no one understands him as completely as I do. Come to think of it, that
could be an illusion — since I have the same feeling regarding most artists. But I must say, if I weren't the Duke of
Cadignan, then I'd like to be such an actor — like. . . .

ALBIN Like Alexander the Great. . . .

DUKE *smiling* Yes — like Alexander the Great. *To Flipotte*
Give me my sword. *He puts it in the scabbard. Slowly* It
really is the most beautiful way of laughing at the world; one
who can play for us whatever he wants, he really is something more than all of us. *Albin looks at him in wonder.*
Don't try to figure out what I'm saying. It's true only for that
very instant I say it. — See you later!

MICHETTE Give me a kiss before you go!

FLIPOTTE Me too!

They cling to him; the Duke kisses both at the same time and exits. — In the meantime:

ALBIN A wonderful person! . . .

FRANÇOIS That is true. . . but that such persons exist is almost a reason not to get married.

ALBIN By the way, explain to me what sort of women these are.

FRANÇOIS Actresses. They're also part of Prospère's troupe, the one who's the innkeeper of this tavern at present. Of course, they didn't do anything much different previously than what they're doing now.

GUILLAUME rushes in, apparently out of breath.

GUILLAUME *goes to the table where the actors are sitting, his hand on his heart, and speaks with great difficulty, leaning on the table* Saved, yes, saved!

SCAEVOLA What's up, what's the matter with you?

ALBIN What's happened to the man?

FRANÇOIS That's play-acting now. Pay attention!

ALBIN Oh —?

MICHETTE, FLIPOTTE *hurrying over to Guillaume* What's up? What's the matter with you?

SCAEVOLA Sit down, have a drink!

GUILLAUME More! More! . . . Prospère, more wine! — I ran! My mouth is all dry. They were at my heels.

JULES *starts* Ah, be careful everyone, they're always at our heels.

PROSPERE So come on, tell us, what happened? . . . . *To the actors* Movement! More movement!

GUILLAUME Women here — women! Ah — *embraces Flipotte* That too brings a man back to life! *To Albin, who is most perplexed* The devil take me, my boy, if I thought I'd see you alive again. . . . *as if listening* They're coming, they're coming! — *To the door* No, it's nothing. — They —

ALBIN How strange! . . . There really is a noise, as if people were rushing by outside very fast. Is that managed from here too?

SCAEVOLA *to Jules* Every time he puts in these nuances. . . it's too silly! —

PROSPERE So tell us why they're at your heels again.

GUILLAUME Nothing special. But if they'd catch me it would cost me my head — I set a house on fire.
During this scene, more young noblemen arrive and take seats at the tables.

PROSPERE *softly* Go on, go on!

GUILLAUME *likewise* Go on with what? Isn't it enough that I set a house on fire?

FRANÇOIS So tell me, my friend, why did you set the house on fire?

GUILLAUME Because the President of the Supreme Court lives in it. We wanted to start with him. We want to take from the good landlords of Paris the desire to invite into their houses people who put us poor devils in prison.

GRAIN That's good! That's good!

GUILLAUME *looks at Grain and is amazed; then continues to speak* Those houses must all have their turn. Three more guys like me and there'll be no more judges in Paris!

GRAIN Death to the judges!

JULES Of course. . . but there may very well be one we can't destroy.

GUILLAUME Him I'd like to meet.

JULES The judge inside us.

PROSPERE *softly* That's absurd. Cut it out. Scaevola! Bellow! Now's the moment!

SCAEVOLA Wine here, Prospère, we want to drink to the death of all the judges in France!

During these last words, enter: the MARQUIS OF LANSAC *with his wife* SEVERINE *and* ROLLIN, *the poet.*

SCAEVOLA Death to all who have power in their hands today! Death!

MARQUIS You see, Séverine, this is how we're greeted.

ROLLIN Marquise, I warned you.

SEVERINE Why?

FRANÇOIS *standing up* What's this I see! The Marquise! Permit me to kiss your hand. Good evening, Marquis! Hello, Rollin! Marquise, you dare come to this establishment!

SEVERINE I've heard so much about it. And besides, we've already had some adventures today — isn't that so, Rollin?

MARQUIS That's right, just imagine, Viscount — where do you think we're coming from? — From the Bastille.

FRANÇOIS Are they still creating such a spectacle over there?

SEVERINE Yes, of course! — It looks like they want to storm the gates.

ROLLIN *declaims*
    Like unto a flood, that surges 'pon the shore,
    And, deeply angered that her very own child,
    The earth, resists —

SEVERINE Don't, Rollin! — We had our coach stop there, nearby. It's a magnificent sight; big crowds really do always have something grand about them.

FRANÇOIS Yes, yes, if only they didn't smell so bad.

MARQUIS And then my wife didn't give me a moment's peace. I had to bring her here.

SEVERINE So what is actually so special here?

PROSPERE *to Lansac* So, you're here too, you dried up old scoundrel? You bring your woman along 'cause you can't be sure enough of her at home?

MARQUIS *forcing a laugh* He is a character!

PROSPERE You be careful she doesn't get snatched away from you here. Fashionable ladies like her sometimes get a goddam itch to try it with a real hoodlum.

ROLLIN I'm suffering unspeakably, Séverine.

MARQUIS My child, I warned you — there's still time for us to leave.

SEVERINE What is it you want? I find it charming. Do let's sit down!

FRANÇOIS Marquise, permit me to introduce the Chevalier de la Tremouille to you. It's his first time here as well. The Marquis of Lansac; Rollin, our famous poet.

ALBIN My pleasure. *Compliments; they all sit down.*

ALBIN *to François* Is she one of those who puts on an act or . . . I have no idea what's going on.

FRANÇOIS Stop being so dense, will you! — This is the real wife of the Marquis of Lansac. . . a most respectable lady.

ROLLIN *to Séverine* Tell me that you love me.

SEVERINE Yes, yes, but don't ask me every single minute.

MARQUIS Have we missed any of the scenes already?

FRANÇOIS Not much. That one over there is playing an arsonist, it seems.

SEVERINE Chevalier, you must be the cousin of the little Lydia de la Tremouille who got married today.

ALBIN Yes, I am, Marquise. That was one of the reasons for my coming to Paris.

SEVERINE I remember having seen you in church.

ALBIN *embarrassed* I am most flattered, Marquise.

SEVERINE *to Rollin* What a nice young boy.

ROLLIN Ah, Séverine, you've never yet met a man you didn't like.

SEVERINE Oh, I did; and him I married right away, too.

ROLLIN Oh, Séverine, I'm always afraid — there are even moments when your own husband is a danger to you.

PROSPERE *brings wine* Here you are! I wish it were poison, but for the time being I'm not allowed to serve that to you swine.

FRANÇOIS The time'll come, Prospère, don't worry.

SEVERINE *to Rollin* What's the matter with those two pretty girls? Why don't they come closer? As long as we're here I want to take part in everything. I find the goings on here to be most civilized.

MARQUIS Just be patient, Séverine.

SEVERINE I find one has the most fun on the street, lately. — Do you know what happened to us yesterday, as we drove along the promenade in Longchamps?

MARQUIS Oh, please, my dear Séverine, why. . . .

SEVERINE A fellow jumped on the running board of our carriage and shouted: Next year you'll be standing behind your coachman and we'll be sitting in the carriage.

FRANÇOIS Ah, that's a bit strong.

MARQUIS Oh God, I don't think one should talk about these things at all. Paris has a bit of a fever right now; it'll pass again soon.

GUILLAUME *abruptly* I see flames, flames, everywhere, wherever I look, red, high flames.

PROSPERE *goes over to him* You're playing a madman, not a criminal.

SEVERINE He sees flames?

FRANÇOIS That's still not quite the real thing, Marquise.

ALBIN *to Rollin* I can't begin to tell you how confused I am by all this.

MICHETTE *comes up to the Marquis* I haven't even said hello to you yet, my sweet old pig.

MARQUIS *embarrassed* She's joking, dear Séverine.

SEVERINE I don't agree. Tell me, little one, how many love affairs have you had so far?

MARQUIS *to François* It is admirable, the way the Marquise, my wife, is able to accommodate herself to any situation right away.

ROLLIN Yes, it is admirable.

MICHETTE Have you kept count of yours?

SEVERINE When I was still as young as you. . . certainly. —

ALBIN *to Rollin* Tell me, Monsieur Rollin, is the Marquise making believe or is she really like that? — I have absolutely no idea what is going on.

ROLLIN Being. . . making believe. . . can you tell the difference so precisely, Chevalier?

ALBIN Quite.

ROLLIN I can't. And what I find so peculiar here is that all apparent differences are suspended, so to speak. Reality turns into play-acting — play-acting into reality. Just take a look at the Marquise. How she's chatting with these creatures, as if she were the same as they. And yet she is. . . .

ALBIN Something entirely different.

ROLLIN I thank you, Chevalier.

PROSPERE *to Grain* So, how did all that happen?

GRAIN What?

PROSPERE The business with your aunt, on whose account you sat in jail for two years?

GRAIN But I told you, I strangled her.

FRANÇOIS He's weak. An amateur. I've never seen him before.

GEORGETTE *enters in haste, dressed like a prostitute of the lowest class* Good evening, kids! Isn't my Balthasar here yet?

SCAEVOLA Georgette! Sit with me! Your Balthasar will still arrive in good time.

GEORGETTE If he's not here in ten minutes he'll not come in good time — then he'll not come again at all.

FRANÇOIS Pay attention to this one, Marquise. In reality, she is the wife of this Balthasar she's speaking of just now and who'll come very soon. — She portrays the most common of streetwalkers, Balthasar her pimp. And yet she is the most faithful wife one could find in all Paris.

BALTHASAR *enters.*

GEORGETTE My Balthasar! *She runs to meet him, embraces him* Here you are!

BALTHASAR Everything is in order. *Silence all around* It wasn't worth the effort. I almost felt sorry for him. You should check your people out better, Georgette — I'm fed up with killing promising young men for a few francs.

FRANÇOIS Excellent. . . .

ALBIN What? —

FRANÇOIS He makes his point so well.

The INSPECTOR *enters, in disguise, sits down at a table.*

PROSPERE *goes over to him* You've come at a good time, Inspector. This is one of my most outstanding performers.

BALTHASAR I ought to find a different way of making a living altogether. God, I'm no coward, but the bread I earn this way leaves a bad taste in my mouth.

SCAEVOLA I'll bet it does.

GEORGETTE What's with you today?

BALTHASAR I'll tell you, Georgette; — I think you're a little too affectionate with the young gentlemen.

GEORGETTE See what a child he is. Do be reasonable, Balthasar! I have to be affectionate, you know, to get them to trust me.

ROLLIN What she's saying there is downright profound.

BALTHASAR If ever I were ever obliged to believe that you feel something when another man. . . .

GEORGETTE What do you all say to that! This stupid jealousy will bring him to the grave yet.

BALTHASAR I heard a sigh today, Georgette, and that was at a moment when his trust was already great enough!

GEORGETTE I can't suddenly stop playing the woman in love just like that.

BALTHASAR Take care, Georgette, the Seine is deep. *Wildly* If you deceive me. —

GEORGETTE Never, never!

ALBIN I absolutely do not understand this.

SEVERINE Rollin, this is the right attitude!

ROLLIN You think?

MARQUIS *to Séverine* We can still leave, Séverine.

SEVERINE Why? I'm beginning to feel very good.

GEORGETTE My Balthasar, I adore you. *Embrace.*

FRANÇOIS Bravo! Bravo! —

BALTHASAR What kind of cretin is this?

INSPECTOR This is positively too strong — this is —

MAURICE *and* ETIENNE *enter; they are dressed like young noblemen; however, one can see that they are merely wearing threadbare theatrical costumes.*

FROM THE ACTORS' TABLE Who are they?
SCAEVOLA I'll be damned, if it isn't Maurice and Etienne.
GEORGETTE Of course it's them.
BALTHASAR Georgette!
SEVERINE God, are these young people pretty as a picture!
ROLLIN It pains me, Séverine, that every pretty face excites
    you so violently.
SEVERINE What did I come here for, then?
ROLLIN So tell me, at least, that you love me.
SEVERINE *with a look at him* You have a short memory.
ETIENNE Well, where do you think we're coming from?
FRANÇOIS Listen to this, Marquis. These are a couple of witty
    young fellows.
MAURICE From a wedding.
ETIENNE One has to get dressed up a bit for that. Otherwise
    those damned secret policemen get on your tail right away.
SCAEVOLA Did you make a decent catch at least?
PROSPERE Let me see.
MAURICE *taking watches out of his jacket* What'll you give
    me for these?
PROSPERE For this one here? One louis!
MAURICE I'll bet!
SCAEVOLA It isn't worth any more!
MICHETTE Say, that's a lady's watch. Give it to me, Maurice.
MAURICE What will you give me for it?
MICHETTE Look at me! . . . Will this do? —

FLIPOTTE No, me; — look at me —

MAURICE My dear children, that I can have without risking my head.

MICHETTE You are a conceited ape.

SEVERINE I swear to you, this is no comedy.

ROLLIN Of course not, you have something real flashing through everywhere. That's the charm of it, you know.

SCAEVOLA Say, what sort of wedding was it?

MAURICE The wedding of Miss La Tremouille — she married the Count of Banville.

ALBIN You hear that, François? — I assure you, these are real thieves.

FRANÇOIS Calm down, Albin. I know these two. I've seen their act a dozen times already. Their specialty is the portrayal of pickpockets.

Maurice pulls several purses from his jacket.

SCAEVOLA Well, you can sure be generous tonight.

ETIENNE It was a most magnificent wedding. The entire nobility of France was there. Even the King was represented.

ALBIN *excited* This is all true!

MAURICE *allowing the money to roll across the table* This is for you, my friends, so you'll see we stick together.

FRANÇOIS Props, dear Albin. *He stands up and takes a couple of coins* You see, we get a share too.

PROSPERE Go on, take. . . you haven't earned anything this honestly in all your life!

MAURICE *holds up a garter trimmed with diamonds* And whom shall I give this to?

Georgette, Michette, Flipotte grasp at it.

MAURICE Patience, you sweet little mice, we'll discuss it later. This I'll give to the one who invents a new caress.

SEVERINE *to Rollin* Wouldn't you permit me to join this competition?

ROLLIN You're driving me mad, Séverine.

MARQUIS Séverine, shouldn't we be going? I think. . . .

SEVERINE Oh no. This is wonderful. *To Rollin* Ah, I'm getting in the mood —

MICHETTE How ever did you get a hold of that garter?

MAURICE There was such a crowd in the church. . . and when a woman thinks a man is courting her. . . .
Everyone laughs. Grain has lifted François's purse.

FRANÇOIS *goes over to Albin, with the coins* Nothing but play money. Feel better now?
Grain is about to withdraw.

PROSPERE *follows him; softly* Give me the purse you lifted from that gentleman immediately.

GRAIN I —

PROSPERE On the spot. . . or it'll go badly for you.

GRAIN You needn't get rude. *Hands it over.*

PROSPERE And stay right there. I don't have time now to search you. Who knows what else you've put in your pockets. Go back to your place.

FLIPOTTE I'm going to win the garter.

PROSPERE *to François; tosses him the purse* Here's your purse. It fell out of your pocket.

FRANÇOIS I thank you, Prospère. *To Albin* You see, we're really among the most respectable people on earth.

HENRI *who has already been present for a considerable time, seated in the back, suddenly stands up.*

ROLLIN Henri, there's Henri. —

SEVERINE Is he the one you told me so much about?

MARQUIS Yes, he is. The one people actually come here to see.

Henri comes forward, very theatrically; he is silent.

THE ACTORS Henri, what's bothering you?

ROLLIN Observe his look. A world of passion. I mean, he's playing a man who's committed a crime of passion.

SEVERINE Oh, I do appreciate that very much!

ALBIN But why isn't he saying anything?

ROLLIN He gives the appearance of being in a trance. Just watch. Pay attention. . . he's committed some horrible deed.

FRANÇOIS He is somewhat theatrical. It looks as if he were getting ready to deliver a monologue.

PROSPERE Henri, Henri, where are you coming from?

HENRI I have killed a man.

ROLLIN What did I tell you?

SCAEVOLA Who?

HENRI My wife's lover.

Prospère looks at him; he obviously feels at this instant that it might be true.

HENRI *looks up* Well, yes, I did it, what are you looking at me like that for? That's how it is. Is it all that remarkable? You do all know what sort of creature my wife is; it had to end this way.

PROSPERE And she — where is she?

FRANÇOIS You see, the innkeeper is playing along. Notice how natural that makes the whole thing.

Noise outside, not too loud.

JULES What's that noise out there?

MARQUIS Do you hear that, Séverine?

ROLLIN It sounds as if troops were marching by.

FRANÇOIS Oh no, that's our dear people of Paris. Just listen how they're bawling. *Unrest in the cellar; outside it becomes quiet.* Go on, Henri, go on.

PROSPERE Tell us, Henri! — Where is your wife? Where have you left her?

HENRI Oh, I'm not worried about her. She won't die from it. Whether it's this one or that one, what do women care? There's a thousand other handsome men still running around in Paris — whether this one or that one —

BALTHASAR May they all fare so who take our women from us.

SCAEVOLA All who take from us what belongs to us.

INSPECTOR *to Prospère* These are inflammatory speeches.

ALBIN This is terrifying. . . these people are serious.

SCAEVOLA Down with the profiteers! I'll bet the guy he caught with his wife was one of those damned dogs who also steal our bread from us.

ALBIN I propose we leave.

SEVERINE Henri! Henri!

MARQUIS I say, Marquise!

SEVERINE Please, dear Marquis, ask the man how he caught his wife. . . or I'll ask him myself.

MARQUIS *hesitating* Say, Henri, how was it you managed to catch your wife?

HENRI *who was lost in thought for a long time* Do you know my wife? — She is the loveliest and lowliest creature under the sun. — And I loved her. — Seven years we've known each other   . . . but only since yesterday has she been my wife. During these seven years there wasn't a day, not a single day when she didn't lie to me, because everything about her lies. Her eyes just like her lips, her kisses just like her smile.

FRANÇOIS He's hamming it up a bit.

HENRI Every young man, every old man, everyone who attracted her — and everyone who paid her, everyone, I believe, who wanted her, had her — and I knew it!

SEVERINE Not every man can say that of himself.

HENRI And for all that, she loved me, my friends; can any of you understand that? She always came back to me — from wherever she was, back to me — from the handsome ones and the ugly ones — the smart and the stupid, the scoundrels and the cavaliers — always back to me. —

SEVERINE *to Rollin* If only you men had the slightest inkling that it's precisely this coming back that is love.

HENRI What I suffered. . . . Torments, torments!

ROLLIN This is heart-rending!

HENRI And yesterday I married her. We had a dream. No — I had a dream. I wanted to get away from here with her. To solitude, to the country, to an overriding peacefulness. We were going to live like other happily married couples — we dreamed about a child too.

ROLLIN *softly* Séverine.

SEVERINE Well, yes, it's all right.

ALBIN François, this man is telling the truth.

FRANÇOIS Certainly, the love story is true, but we're concerned with the story of the murder.

HENRI I was one day late. . . she had forgotten one, otherwise — I believe — she hadn't wanted anyone else. . . but I caught them together. . . and it's all over for him.

THE ACTORS Who? . . . Who? How did it happen? . . . Where is he? — Are they after you? . . . How did it happen? . . . Where is she?

HENRI *ever more excited* I escorted her — to the theater. . . it was supposed to be the last time today. . . I kissed her —

at the door — and she went up to her dressing room and I left like one who has nothing to fear. — But by the time I had gone a hundred paces it had begun. . . inside me. . . you understand me. . . a tremendous uneasiness. . . and it was as if something forced me to turn around. . . and I turned around and went back there. But then I felt ashamed of myself and went away again. . . and again I was a hundred paces from the theater. . . then it gripped me. . . and again I went back. Her scene was over. . . she doesn't have much to do, you know, just stands on the stage a while, half naked — and then she's finished. . . I stand outside her dressing room, I put my ear to the door and hear whispering. I can't make out a single word. . . the whispering dies down. . . I push open the door . . . *he roars like a wild animal* — it was the Duke of Cadignan and I murdered him. —

PROSPERE *who finally believes it to be true* Madman!

Henri looks up, stares blankly at Prospère.

SEVERINE Bravo! Bravo!

ROLLIN What are you doing, Marquise? The moment you call out "Bravo!" you turn everything back into a theatrical performance again — and the pleasant creepiness is over.

MARQUIS I don't find the creepiness all that pleasant. Let's applaud, my friends, only that way can we free ourselves from this spell.

PROSPERE *to Henri, during the tumult* Save yourself, Henri, run!

HENRI What? What?

PROSPERE Let it be enough now, and see to it that you get out of here!

FRANÇOIS Quiet! . . . Let's hear what the innkeeper's telling him!

PROSPERE *after reflecting briefly* I'm telling him he should get out before the watch at the city gates are notified. The handsome Duke was a favorite of the King's — they'll break you on the wheel! You should have stabbed that slut of a wife of yours, rather!

FRANÇOIS What playing to each other. . . . Splendid!

HENRI Which one of us is mad, Prospère, you or I? — *He stands there and attempts to read Prospère's eyes.*

ROLLIN It's marvelous; we all know he's acting and still, if the Duke of Cadignan were to come in now, he would appear to us to be a ghost. *Noise outside, ever louder. People come in, yelling can be heard. At their head, Grasset, then others, among them Lebrêt, crowding down the stairs. Calls can be heard: Liberty, Liberty!*

GRASSET Here we are, kids, in here!

ALBIN What's this? Is this part of it?

FRANÇOIS No.

MARQUIS What's this supposed to mean?

SEVERINE Who are these people?

GRASSET In here! I tell you, my friend Prospère always has a barrel of wine left over — *noise from the street* — and we've earned it! Friend! Brother! We have 'em! We have 'em!

CALLS OUTSIDE Liberty! Liberty!

SEVERINE What is it?

MARQUIS Let's get out of here, let's get out of here, the mob is approaching.

ROLLIN How do you propose to get out of here?

GRASSET It has fallen, the Bastille has fallen!

PROSPERE What that you're saying? — Is he telling the truth?

GRASSET Can't you hear?

Albin is about to draw his sword.

FRANÇOIS Stop that right now, otherwise we're all lost.

GRASSET *staggering down the stairs* And if you hurry you can still see a merry sight outside. . . the head of our dear Delaunay atop a very long pole.

MARQUIS Is that fellow crazy?

CALLS Liberty! Liberty!

GRASSET A dozen heads we've chopped off, the Bastille is ours, the prisoners are free! Paris belongs to the people!

PROSPERE Listen! Listen! Paris belongs to us!

GRASSET Look how he finds his courage now. Yes, go on and shout, Prospère, nothing can happen to you any more now.

PROSPERE *to the nobles* What do you say to that? You rabble! The joke is over.

ALBIN Didn't I say so?

PROSPERE The people of Paris have won.

INSPECTOR Quiet! — *Laughter* Quiet! . . . I forbid the continuation of the performance!

GRASSET Who is this simpleton?

INSPECTOR Prospère, I'm holding you responsible for all the inflammatory speeches —

GRASSET Is the fellow crazy?

PROSPERE The joke is over, don't you understand? Go on, tell them, Henri, now you can tell them! We'll protect you. . . the people of Paris will protect you.

GRASSET Yes, the people of Paris.

Henri stands there, staring.

PROSPERE Henri really did murder the Duke of Cadignan.

ALBIN, FRANÇOIS, MARQUIS What is he saying there?

ALBIN *and others* What does this all mean, Henri?

FRANÇOIS Henri, speak, won't you?!

PROSPERE He found him with his wife — and he has killed him.

HENRI It isn't true!

PROSPERE You needn't be afraid anymore now, now you can shout it out to the world. I could've told you an hour ago that she's the Duke's lover. By God, I was on the point of telling you. . . . You, Screaming Pumice, we knew about it, isn't that right?

HENRI Who saw her? Where was she seen?

PROSPERE What do you care about that now! The man's crazy — you killed him, you can't do any more than that, can you?

FRANÇOIS For heaven's sake, is it really true, then, or not?

PROSPERE Yes, it's true!

GRASSET Henri — you shall be my friend from this moment on. Long live liberty! Long live liberty!

FRANÇOIS Say something, Henri!

HENRI She was his lover? She was the Duke's lover? I didn't know it. . . he's alive. . . he's alive. —
Tremendous stirring.

SEVERINE *to the others* So, where does the truth lie now?

ALBIN For God's sake!

THE DUKE *forces his way through the crowd on the stairs.*

SEVERINE *who sees him first* The Duke!

SEVERAL The Duke!

DUKE Well, yes, what is it?

PROSPERE Is it a ghost?

DUKE Not that I know of! Let me through!

ROLLIN What do you want to bet it's all prearranged. Those fellows there belong to Prospère's troupe. Bravo, Prospère, a great success!

DUKE What's going on? Are you still playing here, while outside. . . . Don't you know, then, what's going on out there? I've seen Delaunay's head being marched past on a pole. Say, why are you looking at me like that — *steps down* Henri —

FRANÇOIS Beware of Henri.

Henri rushes at the Duke like a madman and stabs him through the neck with his dagger.

INSPECTOR *standing up* This is going too far! —

ALBIN He's bleeding!

ROLLIN A murder has taken place here!

SEVERINE The Duke is dying!

MARQUIS I am dismayed, my dear Séverine, that I had to bring you to this place today of all days!

SEVERINE Why? *with difficulty* It's turning out wonderfully well. It's not every day one gets to see a real duke really murdered.

ROLLIN I still can't grasp it.

INSPECTOR Silence! — No one is to leave the premises! —

GRASSET What's he want?

INSPECTOR I arrest this man in the name of the law.

GRASSET *laughs* It's we who make the laws, you fools! Out with the rabble! Whoever kills a duke is a friend of the people. Long live liberty!

ALBIN *draws his sword* Make way! Follow me, my friends!

LEOCADIE *rushes in and down the stairs.*

CALLS Léocadie!

OTHERS His wife!

LEOCADIE Let me in here! I want to be with my husband! *She comes to the front, sees, cries out* Who did this? Henri! *Henri looks at her.*

LEOCADIE Why did you do it?

HENRI Why?

LEOCADIE Yes, yes, I know why. Because of me. No, no, don't say because of me. I haven't been worth that in all my life.

GRASSET *begins a speech* Citizens of Paris, let us celebrate our victory. Chance has led us on our way through the streets of Paris to this amiable innkeeper. It couldn't have turned out any better. Nowhere can the cry, "Long live liberty" sound more beautiful than over the corpse of a duke.

CALLS Long live liberty! Long live liberty!

FRANÇOIS I think we'll be leaving — the people have gone mad. Let's go.

ALBIN Shall we leave them the body here?

SEVERINE Long live liberty! Long live liberty!

MARQUIS Are you mad?

THE CITIZENS, THE ACTORS Long live liberty! Long live liberty!

SEVERINE *at the head of the nobles, moving towards the exit* Rollin, wait outside my window tonight. I'll throw the key down, like the other night — we'll spend a beautiful hour together — I feel pleasantly excited.

Calls: Long live liberty! Long live Henri! Long live Henri!

LEBRET Look at them — they're running away from us.

GRASSET Let them go for today — let them go. — They won't escape us.

Curtain

MARIONETTES

Three One-Act Plays

I. THE PUPPETEER

A Study in One Act

CHARACTERS

GEORG MERKLIN
EDUARD JAGISCH, *oboist*
ANNA, *his wife*
THEIR SON, *eight years old*
A MAID

A modestly but comfortably furnished room. Two windows, with a view of rooftops, hills, and a pale blue spring sky. Entrance door on the right, another door to the left.

EDUARD JAGISCH *enters from the right. A slender, beardless man of about forty, modestly and neatly dressed; his bearing is a little self-conscious yet amiable.* Right behind him GEORG MERKLIN, *around fifty, with a rather gray beard and thick gray hair; he is wearing a worn-out overcoat with its collar raised, dark trousers shining somewhat with grease spots, a soft hat, and dusty, worn shoes, but his appearance shows a degree of both inner and outer distinction.*

EDUARD Well, here we are, home. Come in, Georg, and welcome. I can't begin to tell you how grateful I am for this coincidence, how very glad I am. . . . *He lays his coat and hat on the sofa* So. — Won't you take your coat off?

GEORG *holds fast to his overcoat with some purpose* Thank you, thank you.

EDUARD *looks at Georg's clothes; an expression of pity passes over his face, one which he does not want Georg to notice* Yes, you're right, it is a bit cool. But of course, we don't have heat any more at the end of April — right? Won't you sit down? *Georg remains standing* Well, Georg, and do you know how long it's been? Over eleven years. . . yes, indeed, we haven't seen each other in over eleven years. And the strange thing is, it was eleven years ago just yesterday.

GEORG Yesterday?

EDUARD Yes, I know it was exactly on the twenty-eighth of April. You see, that evening we were together for the last time has remained unforgettable for me, so to speak, and its memory still holds a rare magic for me.

GEORG Far off.

EDUARD And then such a long time goes by during which we knew nothing of each other — and then, by chance, we run into each other on the street. And we could have lived our entire lives this way, in the same city, without running into each other.

GEORG To be sure.

EDUARD But through no fault of mine. Because for my part, I looked for you, I downright searched for you, at least during the past three years, since I've been back from America. It was very important to me to find you again.

GEORG *who remains rooted to the same spot, looks around the room; then, indifferently* Why?

EDUARD Why? I missed you — that's right! Can't you understand that? Think back, how much time we spent together in the old days; especially towards the end of my stay in Vienna. In my small room on Nussdorfer Street it was, where you read us your play. . . .

GEORG *at the window* A nice view.

EDUARD Yes, I think so too. That's the reason I moved so far out. In spite of its having its inconvenient side at times, especially when I have to ride home from the opera late at night in bad weather. When it's nice out I walk sometimes, even in winter. It really doesn't take more than forty-five minutes. And in exchange I live just about in the country. There's even a small garden next to the house; although we're not permitted to set foot in it, still, it is an advantage for the child, that he need only stick his head out the kitchen window for the smell of the flowers. . . .

GEORG *turns towards him suddenly* You're married?

EDUARD *somewhat alarmed that he has given himself away too soon* To be sure, that I am.

GEORG Say, why don't you tell me that right away?

EDUARD Actually, I wanted to surprise you. Yes, hmm. . . well, now it's out.

GEORG For a long time?

EDUARD Well, yes, you might say that. In any event, it's a fact that my wife is just now picking our son up from school, and our son is eight years old — yes indeed.

GEORG Ah!

EDUARD And I can say that I'm happy — completely happy — perfectly happy.

GEORG *shaking his head* Happy. . . . I wouldn't dare throw such a word around so boldly. That may be a way of conjuring up disaster.

EDUARD I no longer fear any disaster.

GEORG You've changed a great deal.

EDUARD *pleased* You think so?

GEORG When I recall what a jittery, intimidated, one can even say pathetic fellow you were back then. . . .

EDUARD Oh!

GEORG Yes, that sums it up: an inhibited, pathetic fellow. And now! . . .

EDUARD Well, I just have the feeling that all my misfortunes are behind me. Nothing bad will come any more. I know it. — Well, yes, death. But that comes to us all. I don't think of it. And I can assure you, death holds no further terror for a man once he has a wife and child who will weep for him. I don't know how you view these things.

GEORG I have neither wife nor child — thus I face death without sympathy. — Why are you staring at me like that? How do you think I look?

EDUARD Good, good — excellent!

GEORG Gray.

EDUARD   Gray. . . well, I'm also starting — just look, here along the temples. And you are almost ten years older than I.

GEORG   I knew a man who had snow-white hair at twenty-seven.

EDUARD   Of course — Merlet! I knew him too. . . snow-white. I still run into him from time to time, but we've become strangers. . . . That's life! — But he was there too, you know, in our company, on that unforgettable evening.

GEORG   *almost to himself* Being gray proves nothing. Nor do the years prove anything. Aren't there people who still become fathers at sixty or seventy — or participate in military expeditions? Can one call such people old? No. Only one thing proves that we are old — death. The hundred-year-olds are not old; old are those who must die tomorrow. *Pointing out the window* That young lady is as old as the hills if she's going to drop dead at the next corner.

EDUARD   *goes over to him* Oh, I thought you saw my wife, that is, she's bound to be back any minute. . . . No, no, it's not her.

GEORG   I would've been sorry for it, too.

EDUARD   Sorry — but why?

GEORG   Well, I have reason to be careful with such remarks.

EDUARD   What do you mean?

GEORG   I want to tell you a story, something that happened to me on a train a few years ago. It was morning, six o'clock, a winter's morning. Across from me sits a man, reclines in the corner and dozes. I don't know him, I've never seen him, he doesn't interest me in the least. Suddenly the thought goes through my head: Die! And I look at him a long while with this thought in mind. He continues to sleep and doesn't stir. I look out the window again at the snowy landscape, as I'm in the habit of doing, and forget the fellow completely. We arrive in Vienna. I stand up, get off, the other man doesn't. The other man remains sitting, motionless. I call people over — they carry him out — he was dead. . . dead. The doctors called it a heart attack.

EDUARD A strange coincidence, surely.

GEORG Coincidence? — Do you know how much happens in the world day after day because someone secretly desired it — or frivolously expressed it? Have you any idea of the mysterious power inherent in people of creative temperament? — I went to a police officer and reported to him the facts of the case. "Put me in jail, Sir," I said, "because I am obviously the one who has murdered this gentleman. What's more, I don't feel the least remorse." But the police officer didn't put me in jail — he looked at me in the same silly way you're looking at me now and dismissed me again.

EDUARD *joyfully* This is the real you! Same old Georg! Georg! — Where can my wife be keeping herself so long, today of all days! How amazed she'll be. . . . After all, you can imagine I spoke of you frequently, Georg. But can't I offer you a cigar?

GEORG Thank you, no, thanks. I don't smoke anymore. I've weaned myself from these superfluous things. No, no, let it be, it wouldn't agree with me any more.

EDUARD As you wish. But sit down at least. And tell me, finally, what you've been doing all this time. I simply can't understand it, that we heard nothing more from you, that you were as good as —

GEORG That I was as good as dead. Well, yes, you might as well say it. I assure you, it doesn't hurt at all, to be presumed dead. And, on the whole, I don't believe anything better can befall people of my sort.

EDUARD But. . . it did appear, at the time — all of us expected . . . . You really were on your way to becoming great.

GEORG What tells you I didn't? Must others notice it, then? If you sold your oboe today, or if your fingers and lips became paralyzed, so that you couldn't play any more — would you be any less a virtuoso than before? Or assume that you didn't want to play any more and simply threw it out the window, your oboe, because its sound didn't satisfy you — would you no longer be an artist then? Or wouldn't you become one only after you had thrown it out the window, the instrument that was so powerless in comparison to the heavenly music in your brain?

EDUARD Powerless — yes! Look, what you're saying here, I've felt it many times.

GEORG Well, I've thrown it out the window, my oboe. — The blockheads yelled out: He has no inspirations! I let them yell. The true artist can never have an inspiration, because he has everything within himself — he has that inner fullness. That's it, that's what matters.

EDUARD I feel as if I'd heard you just yesterday — really! It's inconceivable to me that we're seeing each other for the first time today, — since that farewell party on April 28.

GEORG But it wasn't any farewell party. Only by chance —

EDUARD It was one for me. I already had my contract for Boston in my pocket. Don't you remember anymore? You all drank to my future; you even made a speech. Don't you remember? — Ah, what an evening! I think back to it as to a dream. As if it were the first spring evening I'd ever actually experienced. We sat beneath tall trees, at two long tables which they'd had to push together for us. There were storm lanterns burning on the tables. Merlet, the snow-white one, sat here — Habicht there, the young actor with the fiery eyes — over there that violinist who died that same year. And your lover. . . at the time, was dressed all in white, had dark red roses in her hair — and later, when there were no other people in the garden beside us, she sat at your feet, her head reclining on your knee. Her name was Irene.

GEORG Yes. Her name was Irene. — While we're at it, I remember very well that you didn't exactly have much to complain about that evening.

EDUARD Oh no, definitely not. And did I? I had nothing at all to complain about.

GEORG Did you see her again? I mean, did you actually ever see her again after that evening?

EDUARD *as if he didn't understand* Irene?

GEORG No, no, the other one. The one who sat next to you. The blonde with the babyface. Didn't you see her again?

EDUARD That blonde? No. I did have my contract in my pocket, for Boston. I had to leave a few weeks later in any case. I had signed it. What was I supposed to do with some blonde with a babyface?

GEORG She was a pretty creature.

EDUARD Oh yes, she certainly was pretty. A friend of Irene's, if I recall correctly.

GEORG Yes, I believe they were friends, insofar as women can be that. *Looking straight ahead* Eduard. . . .

EDUARD Yes?

GEORG I dare say it was the first intoxicating, so to speak glowing evening you ever experienced?

EDUARD It was a rare evening, most certainly.

GEORG I dare say they were the first tender words you ever got to hear — that evening?

EDUARD You think so?

GEORG Oh, I know so. How often had I heard you sigh that you weren't made for happiness, that you were destined to spend your youth alone and unloved because you were such a shy and nervous fellow.

EDUARD Well, yes, my youth certainly was quite miserable in some regards.

GEORG Until that evening, when someone whispered passionate words to you.

EDUARD *with a cunning look* I'm surprised you still remember that!

GEORG There's a reason for it, Eduard. And I find it very likely that fate has brought us together one more time only in order for you to learn the truth.

EDUARD *as above* What are you trying to tell me, Georg?

GEORG I'd guess that evening was more significant for you than you suspect. I think on that evening you drank in the spirit of life which fills you to this day. Because, admit it, it was then that you felt for the first time that you too are capable of giving happiness, of receiving happiness.

EDUARD I can't say you're wrong there.

GEORG If not for that hour, I dare say you'd have remained for the rest of your life that shy, nervous fellow I knew you for. Maybe you wouldn't even have found the courage to court a woman.

EDUARD *as if convinced* You may well be right there, Georg.

GEORG And how did all this come about? By what means was this extraordinary transformation in your character called forth? By your believing that the pretty girl, who was, after all, seeing you for the first time, fell in love with you at first sight.

EDUARD I did have every reason.

GEORG You had reason to believe it; but you were mistaken.

EDUARD What? Is it possible?

GEORG The whole thing was a profound joke I had contrived.

EDUARD *with dissembled wonderment* A joke?

GEORG Yes. It was a prearranged scheme. The little one who was so tender toward you was simply doing what I wanted. You were the puppets in my hand. I controlled the strings. It was arranged that she would pretend to be in love with you. Because I always felt sorry for you, Eduard. I wanted to awaken an illusion of happiness in you so that true happiness would find you ready once it appeared. And so, as is, perhaps, given people of my sort to do, I may have had an effect more profound, even, than I intended. I made you into a different person. And I suppose I can say it: it is a more exalted pleasure to play with living beings than to cause figures of air to whirl around in poetic dances.

EDUARD Listen, Georg, taking things all in all, I find you shouldn't have told me this.

GEORG Why?

EDUARD Just think, if I had imagined all sorts of things back then; it really would be somewhat embarrassing now. . . .

GEORG Why?

EDUARD *at the window* Ah, there she is! My wife! ah, how glad she'll be!

GEORG Well, I'm sorry to say that I was not prepared. You'll be kind enough to apologize for me to your wife — on account of my clothes.

EDUARD Please, let's not stand on ceremony! You will certainly be welcome to my wife.

ANNA *barely thirty years old, very pretty, dressed very simply but with taste, and the eight-year-old boy enter.*

EDUARD Finally, you're here! Take a look, Anna, whom I've brought home for you.

GEORG *bows.*

ANNA *sees him, recognizes him, is very surprised, composes herself; cordially* Then you're alive!

GEORG *looks up.*

ANNA *extends her hand to him* You are most welcome.

GEORG *has recognized her* Is it possible, then? Anna! *To Eduard* And this person lets me tell my story to the very end. Such a cunning character is what this inhibited fellow turned into. So the two of you got married?

EDUARD Yes, as you see. And now imagine how we've been looking forward to this moment, indeed, how we longed for it in a way. I, and Anna too.

ANNA Yes, me too! *She looks at Georg a long time.*

EDUARD *to Anna* The thing is, you have to know that we were his puppets. We danced on his strings. But they gradually became quite alive, your puppets, right, Georg?

GEORG Yes, I can see that. So this is your son. A pretty child. And how old are you, little man?

THE CHILD Eight-and-a-quarter years!

GEORG And what is your name? *He holds him by the hands.*

THE CHILD My name is Georg Jagisch.

GEORG Georg? *Turning to the others* Georg? Which of your relatives is named Georg?

EDUARD None. We simply ventured to name him after an old friend, after a certain puppeteer — *he laughs, pleased* — It was an idea of my wife's, by the way.

GEORG *looks at them all* Kids, I don't suppose you have the least notion of how trite you are. *To himself* Georg —

ANNA Now, boy, run along, straighten out your things, wash your hands; then you can come in again.

GEORG That's right, Georg, then you can come in again. —
Georg. When another person has the same name we do, and
such a very small individual to boot — there's something
fundamentally comic about that.

THE CHILD *exits.*

EDUARD *and* ANNA *look at each other. Pause.*

ANNA And so we see each other again. Do sit down, won't
you? Won't you take your coat off? *Eduard gives her a
glance* Although it is somewhat cool — actually, I think I'd
like to throw something on myself.

GEORG Yes, it is cool. But aside from that, I want to confess
quite honestly: I'm in my work jacket, which is why I don't
want to take my coat off. I had no idea, you see, that I would
suddenly be appearing as a visitor. — Really, my dear Anna,
how young you've stayed!

EDUARD Do let go of the formality, like before; there is really
no reason —

GEORG There really is no reason. . . . My, Anna, how young
you've stayed!

EDUARD *looking lovingly at his wife* Yes.

ANNA *somewhat embarrassed* But how did it happen, how did
the two of you. . . .

EDUARD Just imagine the coincidence, Anna! Here, in front
of the house! After one has spent years searching for a person
as if with lanterns! I'm going for a walk — or rather, I'm
coming from rehearsal, there I see him, ten steps ahead of me
— from his gait I recognized him — and call out to him.
And he turns around and wants to continue on his way.

GEORG I didn't recognize you, I'm a little shortsighted.

EDUARD Or wanted to get away from me again. But no, that
would really be too bad; when one has spent years searching
for someone —

GEORG *seriously* As if with lanterns.

ANNA Where have you been, actually, all this time?

GEORG Mostly I was traveling.

ANNA Traveling?

GEORG Yes, all over the world.

ANNA And alone?

GEORG By choice, alone. Although not at first.

EDUARD I imagine at first you had Irene — traveling with you?

GEORG Yes, I traveled with Irene.

EDUARD Hmm. Where — I mean — *Anna gives him a look* I wonder where she might be now, Irene.

GEORG *calmly* I don't know. I haven't heard from her in a long time. I roamed far and wide. I've even been in California and in India.

EDUARD Ah!

GEORG Then I gradually confined myself to Europe, and later on my trips grew ever shorter. *Describes a spiral with his hand* — The circle ever narrower. Now I only go on walking tours in the environs of Vienna. But that doesn't change anything. Because for me, a walk in the country out there means more than a trip around the world to others. Because there are human beings and destinies everywhere if one knows how to see and hear.

EDUARD All in all you live a very retired life now, don't you?

GEORG You might say that. I find company too, when it happens to suit me. I have friends too, men and women — for one day. And one day is a long time, when one knows how to live. I'm like Harun al-Rashid, who wandered unrecognized among the people. The people with whom I speak, *broad gesture* out there, have no idea who I am; and whoever says good-bye to me doesn't know whether he'll find me again. It makes for a highly interesting existence.

EDUARD And when you don't go for a walk, what do you do with yourself then? How do you occupy yourself? *With a sudden decision* Are you still writing?

GEORG Writing. . . . In the sense in which you use the word — no! In a different one — yes.

EDUARD I knew it!

GEORG You know nothing! You are, in any case, familiar with the fact that one must eat — at least once in a while. For that reason only I occasionally write short pieces for a magazine. Not under my name, of course. I could just as well carry coal or whittle pipe stems. By which I mean to say that this work has nothing to do with my soul, it does not rob me of any inner freedom. But enough about me! Enough! *Pause. Anna and Eduard exchange a glance.* It's strange.

EDUARD What do you find strange?

GEORG How the two of you are living here in a comfortable house; the lamp hanging above the table, a child growing up — *the maid enters* A maid waits on you. You're probably also insured against accidents and fire —

ANNA *takes the tablecloth from the maid's hand and begins to set the table herself. The maid exits.*

GEORG Now who would have foreseen this ten years ago?

EDUARD Yes, indeed, who would have foreseen this, eleven years ago April 28!

GEORG *as if recalling something* Only, I don't understand how all this came about. It was a joke, after all.

EDUARD But out of it came something serious. Isn't that right, Anna? *He puts his arm around Anna's waist; she, who is in the process of setting the table, repels him gently* Something wonderfully serious.

GEORG But how did it come about, that the two of you —

EDUARD Just think about it, Georg. I'd say that was the least she owed me.

ANNA Don't say that, Eduard! — Had it been no more than my obligation, I would have paid that off simply by confessing the truth to you.

GEORG *looks from one to the other* I see — now everything is clear to me.

EDUARD You're very much mistaken there! Because you don't know the most interesting part yet, not by a long shot!

GEORG And that might be?

EDUARD The really interesting part of the entire affair is that Anna had a soft spot in her heart for you earlier on.

GEORG For me? I see. I suppose that a joke is to be played on me now.

EDUARD A joke? That wouldn't be bad. *Returning Anna's glance* Oh, let him know everything. We owe it to him. In many respects. That's right, she had a soft spot in her heart for you.

GEORG Anna —?

ANNA *setting the table, calmly* I suppose it must have been something of the sort. Otherwise I'd hardly have agreed to take part in the entire charade.

GEORG This I don't understand. I don't understand a single word.

ANNA This charade, you see, was my last hope, so to speak. You were supposed to become jealous.

GEORG I was supposed to —? I see. . . . Hmm, Eduard, say, this must be unpleasant for you to hear, isn't it?

EDUARD Unpleasant? For me? You really are funny. Can't you tell that I'm just now experiencing the greatest triumph of my life?

GEORG Well, yes, if that's how it is, — then do go on with your story, Anna.

ANNA There is nothing more to tell. *Smiling* My scheme failed, as you know. You absolutely did not become jealous. And so, it was simply over.

GEORG Over. . . .

ANNA *smiling* It pretty well had to be over, since the last hope failed. Right? At that point, I had to come to terms with it, naturally.

GEORG Nevertheless, one must also consider the possibility that your soft spot for me wasn't worth all that much.

EDUARD I always maintained that, for my part. It was more a kind of friendship she felt for you, sympathy, if one may say so. And therefore it was important to her to bring you onto the right path again.

GEORG Onto the right path —?

ANNA The one I took to be the right one.

EDUARD For that it was necessary, first of all, to cure you of a disastrous passion.

GEORG Of what passion?

ANNA *stares straight ahead.*

GEORG Of what disastrous passion?

EDUARD *remains silent.*

GEORG Irene —? *Pause* — Irene —?

ANNA It was partly her fault, so to speak, that you gave up your settled existence back then, after your first success —

EDUARD That you resigned the position from which you were still receiving your secure income —

GEORG She believed in me! She believed in me. She didn't want me to tie down my free spirit in the bonds of a daily occupation.

ANNA I wanted so much to see you enjoy security and peace, and I was afraid that you would never find them with Irene.

GEORG Security? Peace? Are these things that ever held any value for me?

ANNA Well, anyway, at the time, some people thought Irene wasn't quite the right one for you.

GEORG Not the right one?

EDUARD Shall I put it more forcefully? She made a fool of you.

GEORG Me? Irene — me?

ANNA In any event, I was convinced it would be in your best interest if you didn't stay with her. I even felt at times as if you yourself sensed —

GEORG As if I myself sensed —?

ANNA As if you yourself sensed that Irene wasn't — That is why I took part in that charade. It even appeared to me at one point that evening that the game would succeed. . . . You looked at me so strangely from time to time. . . .

GEORG How did I look at you?

ANNA The way you used to look only at Irene. . . . And on the days that followed I imagined all sorts of silly stuff. I was waiting for you, as it were. I felt as if you'd have to. . . as if . . . . *Pause* But you didn't come. And after I had waited a few days in vain, everything finally became clear to me. Everything. Everything. And I was very much ashamed of myself. Not only for myself; for him as well. For Eduard. Yes, truly, to the depths of my soul I was ashamed — for both of us. I was so hurt. What I wanted most was to —

EDUARD No, don't say it!

ANNA *quietly* . . . was to die. . . .

EDUARD Yes, she told me that too at the time, Georg. And she fell to her knees before me. . . . That is to say, I raised her up at once, of course. . . . and she confessed everything to me, everything. Indeed, much more than you yourself knew. And in my arms she cried herself out.

ANNA *smiling* Yes. And thus it was made good again, too. It didn't take all that long. It was quite good after all, I soon thought, that he hadn't come.

EDUARD And she wrote me letters while I was over in America. Oh, and what letters! I've saved them all. We read them together once in a while. They're in the drawer over there. And then, after a time, she bought a ticket and took a ship and came to me in Boston. Yes, Georg, you see standing here a human being who followed me to America, so very much did she — love me. *Pause.*

GEORG *reflecting* And if I had come, back then, when you were waiting for me?

ANNA Then a number of things would have turned out differently, most likely.

GEORG It may well be. What dangers one is sometimes threatened by without suspecting it!

EDUARD How so?

GEORG If I consider, it could have happened to me, to become a settled family man, like you — to sit under a hanging lamp and have a maid to wait on me. . . . No, let's all be glad I didn't come back then. No, I wasn't born to dine at a table set with a white cloth.

EDUARD But today, Georg, today you will do so for once, won't you?

GEORG What?

EDUARD You'll stay here for dinner.

GEORG Absolutely not.

EDUARD But look, Anna already set a place for you.

GEORG No — please — stop that. I do not wish to be disturbed in my life's routine. I am no longer young enough to put aside habits of many years standing.

EDUARD What habits are we talking about here?

GEORG It's my habit — you may smile about all you want — to have my dinner in the open, when I feel like it, during one of my walks — and therefore, generally, for the sake of convenience, I carry it with me in my pocket.

THE CHILD *coming in* Isn't the soup ready yet?

GEORG Patience, my young man. It'll be here right away. And since I don't wish to disturb you in your habits either, you'll permit me most humbly to take my leave.

EDUARD But Georg, what can you be thinking of?

GEORG *determined* Let me be.

EDUARD *instructed by a glance from Anna not to insist* Fine, but we will see each other again. . . .

GEORG It's possible, but not certain. Let's leave it to chance. I live in accordance with no program. And if you happen to learn where I live — I set no store by formalities, I expect no return visit.

EDUARD Yes, but even if you don't want to be visited, my dear friend — don't hold my saying this against me — it is possible that. . . you see, I have certain connections — in the end I could be of some service to you.

GEORG Some service? — It seems you want to get me something like a job?

EDUARD Well, it wouldn't be the worst thing.

GEORG I don't suppose you can bear to see me live so free and unrestricted, can you? I suppose I should turn back into a simpleton, like I was back then, when the blockheads held me in high esteem? But times have changed. When I was poor,

I could give you whatever I owned — today I am too rich to be a spendthrift.

EDUARD I'm not thinking of a job in the usual sense, you know. But it might be possible for you, with a degree of peace, with the slightest degree of industry, indeed, without willing it, to achieve fame and fortune.

GEORG Fame? — Ten years — a thousand years — ten thousand? Tell me in what year immortality begins, and I'll be concerned about my fame. — Fortune? — Ten gulden — a thousand — a million? — Tell me what it costs to buy the world, and I'll strive to make a fortune. For the time being, the difference between poverty and wealth, between obscurity and fame is too small to make it worth my while to move so much as my little finger. Let me go for a walk, friend, and play with people. That is the only thing worthy of a man like me. Good-bye, dear friends, I'm glad to have seen you again. *To the little one* Good-bye — Georg — Good-bye! *To the others* Who knows what this little boy is destined to become? And when, at the same time, I think that he would never have been born if I hadn't had the idea, that evening. . . . You must tell him one day, when he's old enough to understand it.

EDUARD That's something we'll want to think about.

GEORG A child of my fancy — truly. *The maid brings the soup.* Good-bye.

EDUARD And not a spoonful of soup — it's downright insulting! You want to leave without the least. . . .

GEORG Well, then, if you must absolutely offer me something, allow me to give my young namesake a kiss on his forehead. *He picks him up and kisses him. After a pause* This sentimental impulse requires an explanation perhaps. Well, I have no reason to keep it a secret from you that I too had a wife once.

EDUARD You had a — wife?

ANNA Irene!

GEORG Yes. And a child as well.

ANNA *stirred* A son?

GEORG Yes.

ANNA Where are they —?

GEORG My wife left me later on, and the boy she left behind with me. . . *purposely coldly* died. Yes. Learn from this, friends: fate does not wish me to be chained to the ground by everyday concerns. People like me must be free if they're to live life fully. Farewell. *Exits.*

EDUARD Georg! *Begins to follow him.*

THE CHILD *has begun eating his soup.*

ANNA Leave him alone! Leave him alone! Let's not take from him the last thing he has left.

EDUARD What do you mean? *Looks at her.*

ANNA *ties a napkin around the child.*

EDUARD *goes over to her, strokes her hair.*

ANNA *does not look up.*

EDUARD *nods, as if understanding* Well, yes. . . .

They sit down to eat.

Curtain

II. THE GALLANT CASSIAN

Puppet Play in One Act

CHARACTERS

MARTIN

SOPHIE

CASSIAN

A SERVANT

A garret in the style of the late seventeenth century. A small German city. View through the window of roofs and towers and, further in the distance, of a hilly landscape lying in the reddish glow of the evening sun. The room is in some disorder. An open chest. An open, half-emptied wardrobe. Linens and articles of clothing are lying about on chairs. MARTIN is busy packing a traveling bag. SOPHIE is standing close to him.

MARTIN Don't cry, child, — don't cry.

SOPHIE But I'm not making a sound.

MARTIN *without turning around* I can tell from your breathing that you're crying.

SOPHIE Shall I help you?

MARTIN That you could do. Look, there in the wardrobe — all the way at the top — there are some handkerchiefs.

SOPHIE *goes over* New ones. . . silken. . . .

MARTIN Give them to me. I hope you don't hold it against me that I'm taking some new silk handkerchiefs on my trip.

SOPHIE And the magnificent lace ruffle! . . . So you did buy it from the Persian merchant after all.

MARTIN Certainly. Or did you want your sweetheart to dress like a journeyman while on his travels? . . . So hand it to me, the ruffle. *Sophie brings it to him slowly. — He points to it* Isn't this another tear?

SOPHIE *simply* I'm sorry.

MARTIN There, there. . . . *good-naturedly; he lightly touches the ruffle with his lips* Now you can see I'm not angry with you. But do calm down now. You'll have to put up with it. *Busy* It's not forever, you know.

SOPHIE I should hope not.

MARTIN Well, then.

SOPHIE But for how long? . . .

MARTIN How long? Do you want to turn me into a liar against my will, child? I don't know how long.

SOPHIE It's the end of March.

MARTIN I know.

SOPHIE The violets were blooming in the meadow beyond the city walls, when we walked out there the other day.

MARTIN What of it?

SOPHIE Will you be here again when the lilac blooms?

MARTIN Maybe sooner. . . maybe a little later too. In the end, not until the peaches turn ripe — what do I know! In any case, I'll come back as long as I stay alive — and that I hope to do.

SOPHIE *anxiously* If you let yourself be recruited, Martin —

MARTIN Recruited? . . . I wouldn't dream of it. I've no desire at all to fight. That's not my cup of tea.

SOPHIE But wait till you're gone! I've heard how well they know to tempt a man, with craft and guile! — And your cousin Cassian, of whom you tell me so much, he is a soldier too, after all.

MARTIN The gallant Cassian — yes, it's different with him. He already beat two robbers to death at thirteen. . . . Oh, a human life is of no more value to him than the existence of a gnat. Quite a character!

SOPHIE I'd like so much to meet him.

MARTIN Cassian! . . . There's a hero! I'll bet sooner or later he'll be made a colonel, general. . . field marshal. . . My, if I were Cassian I'd have long since conquered myself a dukedom. We'll soon hear something of the sort, that's for sure. . . . Of course, the gallant Cassian! — I, however, am a peaceful fellow and play my flute.

SOPHIE And if they offer you a handsome signing bonus?

MARTIN Bonus? . . . Am I some poor wretch?

SOPHIE Soon there won't be much left of all the ducats you've won, Martin, if you keep carrying on so.

MARTIN I'd really get far with the thousand ducats. The paltry thousand ducats I won from the students here! This pack of beggars in town here!

SOPHIE Do you know what they're saying?

MARTIN I can well imagine.

SOPHIE That you're in league with the devil.

MARTIN To them, any wit and good fortune are deviltry. You'll all get the surprise of your lives yet! *Paces back and forth, continuing with his toilette.*

SOPHIE Oh, Martin, Martin!

MARTIN What do you want?

SOPHIE Stay home! Stay home! I have a feeling, you won't stay faithful to me!

MARTIN *embarrassed* Have I ever given you cause to think that?

SOPHIE What do I really know about you? You came to our city only last fall, and you kissed me for the first time on Christmas day.

MARTIN Well, what else? You've learned a number of other things since then! —

SOPHIE Was it the first kiss for you? As it was for me?

MARTIN That I can swear to you.

SOPHIE Martin! . . . And those beautiful women who danced in the ballet here last fall, you didn't kiss any of them?

MARTIN Not one.

SOPHIE Didn't you go to the theater every evening? Didn't you wait far into the night until they went home — at the little door on the Town Hall Square?

MARTIN Still, I didn't know any of them, didn't speak to any.

SOPHIE And the flower you caught?

MARTIN Enough of these childish stories.

SOPHIE *more urgently* What was her name, the one who threw you the flower?

MARTIN I don't remember.

SOPHIE She danced the role of the captive Athenian maiden that night.

MARTIN That may well be.

SOPHIE How I can see her before me! Her black locks curled over her shoulders like twitching snakes in the snow. All who saw her were mad with delight. And the hereditary prince threw roses down to her on the stage — Oh, I still remember! And afterwards, hundreds waited for her on the street; and when she came out, the bouquet in her hand, they all shouted with joy, and she smiled, and looked all around her, and strewed flowers among the crowd — And you, you, yes you! — you bent down and chased after one and picked it up from the ground and hid it — I saw it perfectly well! — inside your jacket.

MARTIN *puts his hand automatically to his chest. He casts a hasty glance at Sophie to see whether she noticed.* Well, so what? She's gone, I've heard nothing further from her.

SOPHIE But I'm afraid, Martin, that you could one day forget me and betray me on account of a woman like that.

MARTIN Nonsense! . . .

SOPHIE Keep in mind, Martin, they're all false, those women who wander homeless through the world. . . however beautifully they might dance or sing. And keep in mind, it would be a misfortune for you too if you were to forget me!

MARTIN *impatiently* What time is it?

SOPHIE An hour before sunset, Martin.

MARTIN Three more hours! . . . Three long hours before the stagecoach leaves.

SOPHIE Long? . . . Long? . . .

MARTIN Have I hurt your feelings?

SOPHIE *bursting out* Why. . . why are you going away?!

MARTIN How many more times are you going to ask the same
silly question? Because something is driving me away.. . . .
The blood rushing through me. . . the blooming spring
outside . . . . I want to see something new — people —
cities! . . . The walls in here irritate me — the city walls
entrap me . . . I can't play a single song. . . . *back and
forth; notices Sophie glancing anxiously at him* There's
something so silly about the last hour before saying good-bye!
. . . Don't you have to go home, Sophie? — it's getting late.

SOPHIE If you want, Martin, I'll leave right away.

MARTIN It's not that I want you to, but your mother. . . .

SOPHIE Today I can stay out later. I wanted to accompany you
to the stage.

MARTIN You did? . . . Well, that's fine. So I imagine we can
have dinner together.

SOPHIE Of course.

MARTIN Let's go.

SOPHIE Where to?

MARTIN I think, like the other day, along the river — to the
Golden Swan.

SOPHIE There —?

MARTIN Don't you want to?

SOPHIE As you may well imagine! . . . With the soldiers
there, and the students, with their saucy looks. . . .

MARTIN That's why? That won't bother us much.

SOPHIE How close did you come, recently, to attacking each
other with your swords?

MARTIN It's not my fault. I won't stand for it when someone
looks at you in an unseemly way.

SOPHIE Wouldn't it be cozier staying at home?

MARTIN Cozy it certainly would be. But there is nothing to eat here. Frau Brigitte has been gone since this afternoon, and my servant isn't coming until it's time to take my bag to the coach.

SOPHIE I'll go get something myself.

MARTIN You want to?

SOPHIE A little bit of cold meat, pastry, oranges and dates — is that all right with you?

MARTIN Dear child! What are you going to do now, all these evenings while I'm far away?

SOPHIE Think of you. . . what else shall I do! — *Sad embrace.*

It has grown fairly dark. Heavy footsteps on the stairs. — Both look up. CASSIAN *enters, wearing a fantastic uniform.*

CASSIAN *very loudly and vehemently* Am I in the right place?

MARTIN Cousin Cassian!

CASSIAN Yes, it is I — Where's this voice coming from? — It's my cousin Martin's voice, ringing out to me from the darkness. . . . Greetings, cousin Martin! And a good evening to the lovely miss.

MARTIN Be it ever so dark, he can tell right away whether a miss is lovely.

CASSIAN More a matter of cleverness than a sharp eye . . . . If it were our old aunt Cordula you'd have lit a lamp by now.

MARTIN Light the lamp, Sophie, light the lamp! That you may see the playmate of my childhood, my father's brother's son, the gallant Cassian, face to face!

Sophie has gone up to Cassian and looks at him. They stare in each other's eyes. Only then does she light the lamp.

MARTIN Where from, Cassian? . . . where to? . . . how long are you staying? . . . what brings you here?

CASSIAN Too many questions for one who is hungry, thirsty and tired.

MARTIN I guess you'll have to provide for three of us, Sophie. Hurry up a bit — you know we haven't got much time. . . . Cold meat, pastry, oranges and dates — as you said.

CASSIAN And you said nothing of champagne, Miss? That would be a pity.

SOPHIE I will bring everything you wish.

MARTIN Hurry back!

SOPHIE See you later.

CASSIAN *stretches out on the bed* Excellent! Ah, I would sure love to rest here for twenty-four hours!

MARTIN You needn't get up again, if you like. I'm leaving.

CASSIAN That's fortunate. Then I suppose you'll let me have your room for one night.

MARTIN For as long as you like.

CASSIAN Perhaps also the young lady who's fetching our supper?

MARTIN Here my right to place at your disposal and yours to ask must end.

CASSIAN Oho! a year ago you wouldn't have found so swift an answer.

MARTIN And a year from now I might have, instead of giving you any answer. . . .

CASSIAN Run me through with your sword. Better let me say it myself, otherwise it could come to a bad end. And that would be silly, since I wish to remain good friends with you. Give me your hand.

MARTIN Welcome.

CASSIAN Let me look at you. You've changed. Your bashful, quiet nature is gone. . . the city has cultivated you, as it seems. Are you still going to church?

MARTIN Oh, Cassian, life itself has enough heaven and hell! — What do I need church and clerics!

CASSIAN Splendid! Splendid! What has happened to you? Did you steal the Shah of Persia's crown from his nightstand? Are you traveling tomorrow into the far reaches of India in a gilded coach? Have you poisoned the Archbishop of Bamberg and are they on your track? Are you going to Africa on a lion hunt? Has the Sultan invited you to his harem? Or are you, in the end, that rascal who recently, on the highway between Worms and Mainz, ambushed the coach in which the beautiful Countess of Wespich and her beautiful daughter were sitting? Is it you who hanged the driver from a tree and sired on both ladies the children who came into the world in the same hour the day before yesterday?

MARTIN None of those things.

CASSIAN Ah — I sensed it: the girl who's bringing us dates and oranges is a princess in disguise.

MARTIN She hasn't got a thing to do with it!

CASSIAN Damn, there is one person who can arouse Cassian's curiosity. . . and that's my little cousin Martin!

MARTIN Listen, then! . . . *He takes a flower from his doublet* This flower here came from a woman with whom I've not even spoken yet, and whom I love madly. She was here in town this fall, and danced — her name is Eleonora Lambriani — *he staggers.*

CASSIAN What is it?

MARTIN I get dizzy simply from saying her name.

CASSIAN Eleonora Lambriani? . . . The Duke of Altenburg's mistress?

MARTIN Former!

CASSIAN The one who danced nights in the castle park at Fontainebleau for the King of France and his officers without so much as a veil on —?

MARTIN He's a blockhead who doesn't understand it. She was intoxicated by her own beauty.

CASSIAN The one who threw the Count of Leigang out the window into the courtyard so that the dogs threw themselves on him and chewed off one of his ears —?

MARTIN It was only one floor, and he kept the other ear —

CASSIAN The one who once swore to bring bliss to a different lover every night for ninety-nine nights, none of whom could be below the rank of prince, — who kept her vow, and who on the hundredth night fetched a lad from Savoy with his hurdy-gurdy into her bedroom —?

MARTIN Yes, she's the one, she's the one! that miserable, most splendid, most beautiful of women! And I want her — I must have her! And then die!

CASSIAN You want? . . . It could be that you'll get her for a penny; — but it's also possible that she'll demand ten thousand ducats to let you kiss the tips of her fingers. It's possible that she'll tear her chemise in two at your first look of desire — but it can also be that she'll send you up against a thousand Turks before she permits you to undo the buckle on her shoe.

MARTIN I'm ready.

CASSIAN Do you know where she is at this moment?

MARTIN In Homburg. She's dancing there at the festivities taking place in conjunction with the meeting of monarchs. And by tomorrow morning, I'll be there.

CASSIAN Where have you buried your treasures?

MARTIN Today they're still in other people's pockets. But by tomorrow, before evening, I'll be rich.

CASSIAN How do you intend to manage that?

MARTIN Can it be you don't know that all the gamblers of Europe are streaming into Homburg for the festivities? . . . Whoever sits down to play with me, his riches are mine. One day is long enough when one has luck. And in the evening I'll go the theater, sit on stage, see Eleonora dance, and afterwards I'll wait in front of her door and lay my riches, my heart and my life at her feet.

CASSIAN And if she doesn't want to know anything of you?

MARTIN I'll be a corpse by midnight.

CASSIAN Your imagination is going lame too early. At one in the morning I will dance a minuet with her on your grave and the Emperor of China shall watch from a balloon.

CASSIAN You're right to make fun of me, Cassian, since you know only my hopes and wishes, but not my strength and skill. You don't know that I'm bound to win.

CASSIAN Bound?

MARTIN However the dice may fall — they fall in my favor.

CASSIAN You're sure of that?

MARTIN As sure — as I am of my eyes and my hand.

CASSIAN Have you tested them?

MARTIN Naturally. At first I played by myself. When I was sure I knew what I'm doing, I invited some friends over, students like me, one brought another, they all lost, and today I have the money of the entire city in my pockets. It's not all that much, a thousand ducats, but it's enough for my outfit, my traveling expenses, and the first stake.

CASSIAN I can't wait to try it. . . . Are you quite sure it works?

MARTIN Try it then! Here are cup and dice; let's play.

CASSIAN Excellent. *Takes the cup in his hand* But what about the lovely miss who's getting our supper?

MARTIN The poor child! — As you know, Cassian, when I said good-bye to you in the fall, you joined your regiment and I entered the university, I was an innocent boy, had not yet kissed any girl's lips, not sworn love to any. Could I face Eleonora thus? . . . I didn't dare! In Sophie's arms I learned how to kiss, to her I swore the oaths that girls like to hear. I played the passionate, jealous, tender lover, and I know how to do with a woman what I want. One final test is still to come for me to feel victorious, and strong enough so as not to tremble before the woman I worship. Before leaving town I want to tell her that I will never see her again; and you shall bear witness how she flies to this window in all haste in order to throw herself out.

CASSIAN *shaking the dice* Your stake, cousin Martin! — What? Only one ducat?

MARTIN That's how I start.

CASSIAN *rolls the dice* Three.

MARTIN *likewise* Four.

CASSIAN That was really noting special.

MARTIN No more than I needed.

CASSIAN Ten.

MARTIN Eleven.

CASSIAN Twelve. . . . Ha, now you're not going to make it!

MARTIN Twelve.

CASSIAN Damn! — Eleven!

MARTIN Twelve. — Onward!

CASSIAN Onward? I'm finished. I haven't another cent in my satchel. *Sophie enters.*

CASSIAN Gracious Miss, here you see a man who at this moment is as poor as a churchmouse. . . .

MARTIN That you shall not say. . . . Here, my friend, it's one ducat. I'll gladly lend it to you.

CASSIAN *putting it in his vest pocket* One never knows. . . .

SOPHIE *prepares the table, pours the wine* So it's true he has a system with which he's bound to win without fail?

CASSIAN It seems so. . . . Thank you. Your health, Miss. . . your health, cousin Martin. . . . Who would have foretold yesterday that I should be sitting today at a table among friends. . . . My, what a lovely bonnet you have, Miss!

MARTIN Really, it is lovely. You didn't have it on when you left to get the food.

SOPHIE But I live so close by. I ran up to my room for a minute — one does have to fix herself up properly when her sweetheart has such distinguished company.

MARTIN She knows what's becoming, doesn't she?

CASSIAN And what tastes good no less. I swear the truffle pie I ate for breakfast at the Duke of Andalucia's was ridiculous beggar's fare compared to this one!

MARTIN That's hardly possible. . . . Really, it's quite a modest inn that this pie come from, and I don't imagine the cook has ever been beyond the city limits. . . isn't that so, Sophie?

SOPHIE You're mistaken, Martin. Since I was at my house already anyway, I ran across the market square to the Pilgrim Camel — they have a cook there now whom the Grand Duke of Parma chased out of the country because he cooked so well that the Princess absolutely wanted to marry him.

CASSIAN Long live the Grand Duke, the Princess, and the Pilgrim Camel. . . and you, my dear Miss! *They drink.* Delicious! I never would have thought the cellars here to be supplied with such excellent wines.

MARTIN There is no shortage of those in town. What's more, they're as inexpensive as you'll find anywhere. Thirteen cents a bottle — isn't that so, Sophie?

SOPHIE No, Martin. This is the best wine they have at the Pilgrim Camel. It costs a ducat a bottle.

MARTIN Damn! What did they do, give you credit on your pretty face?

SOPHIE No. I left the golden bracelet you gave me recently as security. . . . Shouldn't I have, I mean, since we have such distinguished company. . . ?

CASSIAN My thirst is good, the wine is better — but your hospitality, Miss, is better than thirst or wine. Permit me to kiss your hand, Miss.

SOPHIE Do stop calling "Miss" — you'll make me ashamed. My mother is a poor widow, and my father was an ordinary blacksmith all his life.

CASSIAN You may be able to convince someone of that who understands less of the world and women. . . . Your father was no blacksmith.

SOPHIE I assure you, Sir. . . my mother is a respectable woman.

CASSIAN We will not entertain any doubt, Miss, that your mother was, to the best of her knowledge, virtuous; but I will swear she became infatuated with the pagan goddess Venus who most likely appeared to her in a dream while she was carrying you. That sort of thing happens to the most respectable women; I myself was invited into the dream of a distinguished lady to whom a Moorish prince appeared and who gave birth to a coal black baby girl! *The sound of bells ringing.*

MARTIN *impatiently* The dessert! Time's flying! . . . What? There's nothing else? Ah, Sophie, you forgot something after all, in spite of all your care!

SOPHIE Oh no I didn't! *She brings in a centerpiece with fruit.*

CASSIAN Magnificent! . . . They smell as fresh as if they'd just been picked from the tree.

MARTIN How did you get such splendid fruit? . . . How does such magnificent fruit come to be in this town?

SOPHIE It's a coincidence. I saw the centerpiece displayed in Silvio Renatti's showcase.

CASSIAN Beautiful enough to adorn a princely table.

SOPHIE That's what it was meant for, too. The Mayor is receiving the Prince of Dessau today, who's stopping here on his way through to his encampment. . . .

MARTIN And? . . . Am I the Mayor? . . . Is this the Prince?

SOPHIE No, not that.

MARTIN Or did I give you more jewelry than I remember that you were able to pay for this centerpiece?

SOPHIE Oh no. This bill I paid in a different way.

MARTIN And how, if it's permitted to inquire? —

SOPHIE The young Italian who was standing in the shop asked a kiss for it. . . .

MARTIN And that's how you paid?

SOPHIE Shouldn't I have, since we have such distinguished company?

CASSIAN You've acted nobly and hospitably beyond all measure, Miss. But I swear, even if this fruit has just come from torrid Sicily, if he who picked it perished from sunstroke, he who brought it to Germany died of homesickness, and Prince and Mayor go mad at being deprived of such a dessert, — still the insolent Italian has allowed himself to be overpaid for it a thousandfold, and he shall make atonement for it to me before I leave the city — But now, let's enjoy it. *They eat. Sophie looks at Cassian. Martin watches her. — Silence. Then —*

MARTIN   *to Cassian* From where are you coming, actually?

CASSIAN   From where? . . . Shall I say it in a few words or tell the whole story?

MARTIN   In a few words, if you can.

CASSIAN   It's not that easy to give a report. I've come from a battle in which two horses were shot out from under me and three helmets were shot off my head. Furthermore, I've come out of captivity, during which several gallant comrades starved and were eaten by rats. Further, from a place of execution, where seven men were shot next to me and where I, thought dead, was thrown into a ditch with them, although all the bullets had whistled past me. Further, from the claws of a vulture who mistook me for carrion, like the others at my side who were beginning to decompose, and who let me fall from a mountain's height down to earth, — on to a haystack, fortunately. Further, from a forest where a couple of merchants took me to be a ghost and in their fright left behind all sorts of valuables and cash. Further, from a very merry house, where Croatian, Circassian and Spanish women attacked each other with daggers for my sake and their gallants tried to kill me, . . . so that I fled through the chimney up to the roof and jumped down five stories, . . . to make a long story short, I've come from so many adventures that it would cost another man more effort to make them up than it cost me to survive them.

SOPHIE   Splendid!

MARTIN   Strange! . . . And you escaped out of these thousand dangers — what luck you had! — without injury?!

CASSIAN That's what I would say if I were a braggart, but since I'm not — see here!

SOPHIE I see nothing.

CASSIAN What's that, Miss, you don't see that the nail on my little finger is broken? *He drinks. Sophie looks at him in amazement.*

MARTIN *increasingly angry* Now we know where you've come from . . . but where are you going?

CASSIAN As soon as I've recovered from my injury I'll return to my regiment.

SOPHIE Oh, if only you would take me along!

MARTIN Are you crazy, Sophie?

SOPHIE What more shall I do here? I believe a nimble canteen tender is welcome everywhere in wartime.

CASSIAN Your hand, Miss, — let's shake hands, the matter is settled!

MARTIN What did you put in her wine, Cassian?

CASSIAN What business is it of yours what the young lady does, since you're going off?

MARTIN I advise you not to do it, Sophie — I advise you not to. Think of your mother!

SOPHIE Is your regiment stationed far from here?

CASSIAN It'll take a day and a night to get there, I imagine, Miss.

MARTIN Damn! Damn!

CASSIAN What's up?

MARTIN I'm dying of impatience; where could my servant be? I'll miss the coach!

CASSIAN Is the time hanging heavy for you? — Come, cousin, I don't like idle quarter hours either. . . come on, one more little game!

MARTIN   Ha, with you? . . . You forget you haven't got another red cent.

CASSIAN   Oho! A rich cousin has lent me a ducat, I dare say I may do with that as I please.

MARTIN   By my soul, that you may. And it shall be a pleasure for me to take from you, besides this ducat, doublet, hose, sword and shirt as well.

SOPHIE   Martin, what's gotten into you to treat your guest in so shabby a manner?

CASSIAN   Get the dice!

MARTIN   A sad stake — a pitiful stake! — I'll shake. — Twelve! Now the joke is over, I imagine.

CASSIAN   Hey, I can do that too! — Twelve!

MARTIN   Ten.

CASSIAN   Eleven.

MARTIN   Two.

CASSIAN   Three. — All that?

MARTIN   As you can see. Are you afraid, maybe? — Four.

CASSIAN   Five.

MARTIN   Eleven! — It seems to be turning.

CASSIAN   Twelve.

MARTIN   Onward!

CASSIAN   That won't be enough any more. . . .

MARTIN   Don't concern yourself! . . . Here is my bag, well-packed; there is more in it than you suspect. *They play.* Eleven!

CASSIAN   Twelve! And it belongs to me.

MARTIN   Here — my armoire! . . . here, my bed. . . my bed linen. . . . You'll be paid! Eleven.

CASSIAN   That I will. . . . Twelve! . . . I've won! And now, enough.

MARTIN Enough! . . . One more time — The servant will be here right away. . . one more time, it can't go on this way!

CASSIAN What do you have left to stake?

MARTIN Everything I'm wearing on my body, goddammit! — and the servant. . . and my seat on the coach. . . .

CASSIAN It's not enough.

MARTIN *pointing to Sophie* And her to boot!

SOPHIE Martin! . . . I'll give myself away by myself. *Sits down on Cassian's lap and embraces him.*

MARTIN Scoundrel! Scoundrel! What have you put in her wine? . . . Don't you hear me? I say "Scoundrel"!

CASSIAN *stands up* Ah! Is that how you mean it?!

MARTIN Onward! Onward!

CASSIAN Come, we'll settle this outside the gates!

SOPHIE For heaven's sake! Cassian! Cassian!

MARTIN I don't have the time it takes to go outside the gates. There's room enough here.

CASSIAN As you wish, cousin.

SOPHIE Cassian, shall I lose you again right away! *Cassian laughs.*

MARTIN This is no time to laugh — onward! *They fence.*

CASSIAN Not bad! You've done well. . . another seven or eight years and you'd be a dangerous foe — even if not for me. *Stabs him to the heart.*

MARTIN *sinking* Woe is me! Woe!

SOPHIE *rushing to Cassian* And nothing happened to you?

CASSIAN I'm sorry, cousin Martin. . . .

SERVANT *enters* Here I am, my lord.

CASSIAN Your lord is standing here. Take the bag! . . . Like that! . . .

MARTIN My eyes grow dim! . . .

CASSIAN What was it you told me, cousin Martin? . . .

MARTIN . . . the shadow of death . . . .

CASSIAN What was her name? . . . Eleonora Lambriani — It would be worth the effort to take one more day's leave —

SOPHIE Eleonora Lambriani — what's this?! The Athenian maiden! That was her name! —

MARTIN Yes, you wretch! You wretch! just so you know it! Eleonora. . . here's the flower. . . I've kept it. . . it's the same one. . . you take it, cousin Cassian. . . bring it to her . . . I send her my regards. . . .

CASSIAN By heaven I'll deliver them, and several things besides, which will amuse her even more!

SOPHIE What, you're leaving me for Eleonora Lambriani?

CASSIAN I cannot deny it. But not until tomorrow morning. —

SOPHIE Woe is me! . . . *She rushes over to the window and throws herself out.*

MARTIN *about to go after her, sinks down* Sophie! Sophie! *Cassian rushes after her, out the window.*

MARTIN *to the servant* Woe! Woe! I can hardly move! Go look!

SERVANT The most wonderful thing has happened. The leaping gentleman has caught the leaping young lady in the air and both have arrived safely below. . . .

CASSIAN *roaring from below* Hey! Are you coming today? Servant! The luggage! Quickly! I don't want to miss the coach! And I still have to give an insolent Italian a little thrust between the ribs beforehand.

SERVANT *calls down* Right away, my lord!

MARTIN Hand me my flute before you go. . . . I thank you. — Wait! . . . On your way to the coach, ring the bell at number seventeen, Way of the Cross . . . .

SERVANT Number seventeen. . . .

MARTIN My strength is fading. . . . They should pick up my corpse at midnight. Do you hear me?

SERVANT At midnight. I will order it done, Sir. *Exits.*

MARTIN *plays the flute* It is bitter to die alone when one was still loved, well-to-do, and full of the most splendid hopes a quarter hour before. Truly, it is a bad joke, and I'm actually not at all in the mood to play the flute. *Lets it fall and dies. The posthorn sounds in the distance.*

Curtain

III. THE GREAT PUPPET SHOW

Burlesque in One Act

CHARACTERS

THE DIRECTOR
THE AUTHOR
THE JOVIAL MAN
THE GROUCHY MAN
THE NAIVE MAN
A CITIZEN
HIS WIFE
SECOND CITIZEN
HIS TWO DAUGHTERS
FIRST SCANDALMONGER
SECOND SCANDALMONGER
THE COUNT OF CHAROLAIS
THE MASTER
A WRESTLER
A GENTLEMAN IN THE AUDIENCE
AN UNKNOWN MAN IN A BLUE CLOAK
CITIZENS, SOLDIERS, WAITERS, CHILDREN

CHARACTERS IN THE MARIONETTE PLAY

THE DUKE OF LAWIN
THE DUCHESS OF LAWIN
THE HERO OF THIS PLAY
THE MELANCHOLY FRIEND
THE CHEERFUL FRIEND
LIESL
THE SOMBER CHANCELLERY CLERK,
   her father
LIESL'S FIANCE
     THE COMMENTATOR
A MUTE GENTLEMAN
A SECOND MUTE GENTLEMAN
A DEAD GIRL
A SERVANT
DEATH

In the amusement park section of the Prater. Evening. — A large marionette theater takes up the elevated background of the stage, its lowered curtain inscribed, "The Great Puppet Show." Along the left side, on a slant, a tall, narrow old fashioned Punch and Judy theater. Further to the front, on the left, extending into the wings, a carousel. On the right, running diagonally forward from the rear, a fence, behind which is a restaurant garden which gives the impression of extending into the wings as well; front right, behind the fence, an elevated podium. A piano stands in front of the large marionette theater. The stage is occupied mostly by tables and chairs; nonetheless, the center is left open, so that a fairly wide path leads from the marionette theater to the apron. — A great noise is to be heard as the curtain goes up. Military music is heard in the distance. In front of the smaller theater, in which a performance is just taking place (two small figures are pummeling each other, both are fetched by the devil, etc.), children with their escorts. A heavy woman collects coins from the audience in a tin cup. The carousel is in motion, carrying both children and adults. On the podium to the right, a music hall singer is just finishing her number. Applause. Most of the tables are occupied; the people are eating and drinking. The CITIZEN *and his* WIFE, *the* SECOND CITIZEN *with his* TWO DAUGHTERS, *etc.,* SOLDIERS, CITIZENS, YOUNG WOMEN. *Others are just arriving, among them the* GROUCHY MAN *and the* JOVIAL MAN.*

THE JOVIAL MAN Well, how would it be if we sat here?

THE GROUCHY MAN What's here?

THE JOVIAL MAN Oh, a new show. . . . At least, I don't know it yet.

THE GROUCHY MAN Show? — Could be. . . . New? Remains to be seen.

THE NAIVE MAN *enters with friends* Ah, look here! This is something new, isn't it? Hey, waiter, . . . Beer!

WAITER Yes, certainly. . . certainly. . . .

Two teenage boys distribute playbills to the arriving people. The PIANO PLAYER *begins to play; then the* DIRECTOR, *dressed like a Viennese scamp, enters, places himself on an elevated step in front of the theater and speaks in the manner of a town crier (in Viennese accent, occasionally in forced high German with false stresses).*

DIRECTOR Gentlemen! Here one may see the prize-winning, very latest theater of figures, also known as marionette theater — a theater which is furthermore liable to and will I trust make a visit to any other theater conclusively superfluous. Because a mere look, or even a glance at the playbill will prove that every dramatic desire of our honored audience has been provided for and attended to here in fullest measure. — In this theater appears no less a personage than the Duke of Lawin, a most princely and elegantly garbed personality, as well as his legally wedded spouse, a most modern woman in sensational costume, and if that's not enough, we have on hand the hero of this play, that is, the one to whom the entire action happens, as well as his buddies, of whom one is melancholy, in contrast to the other, who has the honor of being as merry as a lark. If that's not enough, Miss Liesl appears, a sweet young thing, around whom all sorts of things are likely to revolve and happen, and if that's still not enough, her very own father appears, a somber chancellery clerk, and her fiance, also known as her intended, and a character of superior understanding and full black beard, bearing the title of Commentator. If that's not enough yet, there are two gentlemen taking part in today's performance whose business it is to keep their traps shut and are therefore designated as mute by the author. If all that is not enough, we have in stock a wrestler with medals and titanic strength, a dead girl, a liveried servant whose function it is to open doors, and the very latest, which we've just gotten, a Death as Punch, or Punch as Death, through which the ghastly aspects of this drama could and should be obliterated. To remark further: all these ladies and gentlemen speak in verses which are rhymed, mostly, by which means the banner of poesy is held high and by no means renounced. — — Step right in, gentlemen and ladies! We're immediately beginning a new performance which is beginning immediately.

THE JOVIAL MAN This is an amusing fellow.

THE GROUCHY MAN I know him. . . he used to be a merry-go-round attendant . . . Nowadays anyone can become a theater director.

THE JOVIAL MAN Oh, please — a marionette theater!

THE PIANO PLAYER *continues playing.*

AUTHOR *coming forward with the director* For God's sake!

DIRECTOR But what's the matter?

AUTHOR Look, the people are eating! . . . That just won't do! It interferes, you know: then they don't pay attention, you know!

DIRECTOR They might be listening even less if they were hungry.

AUTHOR But that goes against our agreement. I really feel like withdrawing my play!

The curtain of the larger marionette theater goes up. A woodland scene. All the figures are set up in the background; the strings by which they will apparently be directed are visible.

THE NAIVE MAN They're hanging from up there! Oh, that's really good! *To his friends* Take a look!

HERO *steps forward and sings the following verses accompanied by the piano*
I'm acting in this play
The main part is for me,
I am called a hero,
Which I need not be.
He steps back into the row of figures. — The following figures act in a similar fashion.
LIESL
I'm simply still single,
And Viennese is the plot,
They call me sweet young thing,
Whether I am or not.
DUKE
I bet at the races,
At the jockey club too,
I am a Duke by birth,
Not the first, it is true.
DUCHESS
One's not enough for me,
Especially my spouse,
So say I'm demonic,
I've never hurt a mouse.
SECOND CITIZEN *stands up; to his daughters* Come on, girls, this is nothing for you!
FIRST DAUGHTER But father, we don't understand what any of this means.
SECOND CITIZEN Oh, well then, if you don't understand anything, we may as well stay.
THE OTHER FIGURES *in chorus*
We're the character parts,
Not one is a star,

We sing as a chorus
'Cause that's what we are.
The curtain of the large marionette theater falls.
THE NAIVE MAN   That was the first act.
THE JOVIAL MAN   *applauds.*
THE GROUCHY MAN   My, you are in a hurry.
THE JOVIAL MAN   I simply happen to like it.
THE GROUCHY MAN   Wait. . . .
THE NAIVE MAN   Did you see the strings?
AUTHOR   *to the Director*   The mood is pretty good, don't you think?
DIRECTOR   *shrugs.*
The curtain goes up again.

The scene: a room with modern furniture. A desk to the left. A window out to the street; a door right, leading to the anteroom; another left, to the bedroom. — The HERO *of this play is sitting at the desk.* LIESL *hops in, holds her hands before his eyes.*

LIESL
Quickly now, who can it be? Go on, guess!
HERO
Darling mine. . . !
LIESL   Darling I don't know, but yours — yes.
HERO
Oh, let me believe it.
LIESL   I must go now.
HERO
Stay, just one kind word, but one kiss allow!
LIESL
Right, and what else? Look at what I did bring you.
She strews flowers about the room.

HERO
  Well, you really are the sweetest thing, you!
LIESL
  And now I must go.
HERO   So soon?
LIESL   Yes, my friend,
  To work in the shop.
HERO   Just one moment's delay!
LIESL
  Yes, one moment. . . and then like the other day
  The kissing business won't come to an end.
HERO
  Angry with me? *Long embrace.*
LIESL   I must go now, that's plain.
  Good-bye! And on Sunday I'll see you again! *Exits.*
THE GROUCHY MAN Same old story! . . .
THE JOVIAL MAN How's that?
THE GROUCHY MAN Well, the sweet young thing — I've
  had it up to here with her!
HERO *alone*
  See you again. . . and now she's departed
  With no clue that forever we've parted,
  And that I'll nevermore with her, alas,
  Ride out to Weidling or the Semmering Pass.
THE JOVIAL MAN Charming! It makes me feel right at home!
THE GROUCHY MAN Local color!!! You're falling for it.
THE NAIVE MAN *laughs* Weidling! . . . *To his friends*
  Remember? We were out there once and we ate fried chicken.

The COMMENTATOR *enters. He is dressed in black and has
a long, full black beard; formal and serious. He steps to the
front and bows.*

THE GROUCHY MAN Now what sort of get-up does this one have? I ought to know him! . . . This really is in bad taste!

THE JOVIAL MAN Who is it supposed to be, then?

THE GROUCHY MAN I don't know yet. . . . But I'll figure it out all right! . . .

COMMENTATOR
I'm the Commentator — I play my role prettily,
I don't speak at all if I cannot speak wittily.

HERO *annoyed*
And since you have no part in the action,
Try, at least, not to cause a distraction.
The Commentator goes to the rear, leans against the window-sill, and remains standing there.

THE GROUCHY MAN Ah! Now it's turning satiric!
In the course of the remaining action, the Commentator comes forward only occasionally, when he has something to say. The rest of the time he remains totally unmoved by the proceedings. He concerns himself with no one, and the others do not concern themselves with him.

HERO
Thus much of myself will I reveal:
I tend not so much to do as feel,
And say in lieu of any lengthy narration,
I'm naught but the hero of this presentation.
And once this office I have managed,
I will, preferably undamaged,
Be packed away with utmost care
In a box of green enamel ware.
It isn't enviable, this my lot,
Yet, there's one consolation I have got:
I may be just a marionette, that's true,
But still, the box wherein I rest is new.

COMMENTATOR
 Now I ask you, as a matter of conscience,
 Should I not have spoken these lines so fair?
HERO
 Please, I say, will you not take a chair?
 At times a hero too may speak nonsense.
THE SERVANT *enters*
 Your friends, both cheerful and sad, my lord,
 Have just arrived, as you implored. *Exits.*

THE MELANCHOLY FRIEND, *tall, very correct, dressed in dark colors, and* THE CHEERFUL FRIEND, *somewhat corpulent, in a comfortable suit, enter.*

THE CHEERFUL ONE *hopping*
 Oh life of gaiety beyond all reason!
 How I love the waking springtime season!
THE MELANCHOLY ONE
 I enter with dark, premonitory fear —
 For what purpose was I invited here?
COMMENTATOR
 Thus by means of his opening line
 Is each of these two neatly characterized:
 The fool, no matter where he is, feels fine,
 The serious man feels ever exercised.
THE GROUCHY MAN This is getting on my nerves!
THE JOVIAL MAN But he's supposed to. . . that's precisely
 the joke!
THE GROUCHY MAN A bad joke!
AUTHOR *to the director* I get the feeling the people are bored.
DIRECTOR I told you, you ought to get rid of that character.
 As recently as this morning I told you.

AUTHOR Couldn't we, maybe, still —? . . . I'll hurry up and cross out a couple of lines.

DIRECTOR But quickly — quickly — before it's too late.
The author hurries to the rear, appears at the window and whispers something to the Commentator.

HERO
I've asked you here to be my seconds
In a matter that urgently beckons.

THE MELANCHOLY ONE
What? . . . A duel? . . .

HERO   Yes — until one of us fall.

THE CHEERFUL ONE *with one leg in the air*
Whoopee! There's nothing more jolly at all!

THE MELANCHOLY ONE
When is it supposed to take place?

HERO   At dawn.

THE MELANCHOLY ONE
So, by breakfast time you'll be long dead and gone.

AUTHOR *to the director* All done!

COMMENTATOR *coming forward*
Let the king, the beggar die this night,
The living still rejoice in the light.

AUTHOR *grabbing his head* I told him to keep his mouth shut!

HERO *to the melancholy one*
You're sure?

THE MELANCHOLY ONE
            Last night I saw it, while in bed,
You were slain and in your coffin, quite dead.

HERO
A dream!

THE MELANCHOLY ONE

        But mine come true eight days a week.

HERO *to the cheerful one*

  And did you too have such a nice dream? Speak!

THE CHEERFUL ONE

  If what I dreamt last night I were to say,

  They'd ban this play forthwith, without delay.

COMMENTATOR

  Here morality a very faun shall tame,

  Hence virgins may be admitted without shame.

HERO

  An inexplicable twist of fate

  Has brought me to this sorry state.

THE MELANCHOLY ONE

  Explain!

HERO Of blame I'm not entirely free,

  I've seduced many a maiden and wife;

  Still, by the special favor of destiny

  I've always, till now, escaped with my life —

  And now, for a woman who' given me naught,

  For one I never desired nor sought,

  For one I've never yet laid eyes on,

  Must I, my friends, from this world be gone.

COMMENTATOR

  Destiny's vengeance on hidden paths proceeds.

  And no man knows the outcome of his deeds.

THE MELANCHOLY ONE

  Tell me, who is the mysterious dame?

HERO

  The Duchess of Lawin, that's her name.

  Both the melancholy and cheerful friends become very excited and jerk back and forth.

HERO
  What's the matter?
THE MELANCHOLY ONE   The Duchess of Lawin?
THE CHEERFUL ONE *with both feet in the air*
  The wretched hussy!
THE MELANCHOLY ONE What's your concern herein?
THE CHEERFUL ONE
  You know her?
THE MELANCHOLY ONE And you —?
THE CHEERFUL ONE   What's that you say?
THE MELANCHOLY ONE
  We both know her —
THE CHEERFUL ONE Equally well —?
THE MELANCHOLY ONE   It looks that way!
  *The strings become looser, the cheerful and the melancholy
  friends appear unable to keep their upright position.*
THE MELANCHOLY ONE AND THE CHEERFUL ONE
  I want. . . I shall. . . I can. . . .
  They are on the point of collapse and cannot go on speaking.
COMMENTATOR   No more!
  What is all this crying in pain good for?
  If you persist in making this dreadful noise,
  You'll be put back in your box, and goodnight boys!
THE MELANCHOLY ONE *his strings becoming gradually
  more taut*
  We seem to have no luck today.
THE CHEERFUL ONE *likewise*
  Cheer up! There's still another play!
THE NAIVE MAN Did you get that? . . . Those two have the
  principal parts in the next comedy.
HERO
  I've never seen Duke Lawin's wife,

And yet he wants to take my life.
He suspects me of being her lover,
A mistake from which I may not recover,
He slapped my face full saucily, the louse,
And yet I swear: I do not know his spouse!
THE MELANCHOLY ONE
He swears. . .
THE CHEERFUL ONE   So what, I'd swear in his place too,
It's what we men of honor usually do.
HERO
The Duke is waiting, time passes by so!
Pistols — ten paces — I'm ready — let's go!
The cheerful and melancholy friends exit.
THE JOVIAL MAN   This is a biting satire against dueling.
THE GROUCHY MAN   It's not biting me for the time being.
THE NAIVE MAN   I'm curious if the duel will take place.
CITIZEN'S WIFE   *to her husband, the first citizen*   I won't stay
here if there's going to be shooting.
CITIZEN   But sweetie, don't get yourself all excited. . . .
AUTHOR   These artful pauses! . . . *to the Director*   I told you,
this idiot is ruining the whole thing!
THE GROUCHY MAN   If there's another monologue coming
I'm going to become unpleasant.
THE JOVIAL MAN   That won't be very difficult for you.
THE GROUCHY MAN   What's the meaning of this? . . . Are
you the grouchy one or am I!? . . .
HERO
That both my seconds speedily
Recognized their rivalry —
THE MELANCHOLY ONE   *beats on the table,*
HERO
— For the favors of this same Duchess

To whom I am a total stranger,
And for whom I'm to face this mortal danger
I find most mysterious. And such is
My dilemma now: how shall I, poor man, spend
My last few hours before the bitter end?

COMMENTATOR *steps forward*
I see the spring both laugh and beckon,
Still it seems too short for us, I reckon;
Yet he who has but one day left on earth
Can think of nought to do with it of worth.

DIRECTOR Say, why didn't you cut that line?

AUTHOR That's the most beautiful passage!

DIRECTOR Haven't you noticed how the audience is getting
restless? . . . Now just imagine if they were hungry besides!

AUTHOR Animals!

THE NAIVE MAN Look, now he's writing. . . . Ah, that's
good!

HERO *has sat down at the desk and is writing*
All my possessions, darling, I do leave to thee,
Yet ere this day is o'er shall we two wedded be.
To the audience
For, if I left her without this estate,
Her father would kill her (a deadly fate),
Since he is a gloomy clerk
From a very old box, a jerk
With little concept of good and evil
Who understands nothing of life, the devil.
Doorbell rings.

THE SERVANT *enters*
The bell rings, I opened the door, it's my duty,
And come face to face with this demonic beauty. *Exits.*

DUCHESS *enters; with grand gestures.*
  Duchess of Lawin is my name,
  A seeker after sensuous game.
  The Duke will shoot you tomorrow — bang! bang! You die!
  But today, at least, you'll learn the reason why.
  She locks the door.
THE NAIVE MAN Now she's even locking the door! Pay
  attention, kids, this could get good now!
HERO
  What are you doing?
DUCHESS   Your hours are numbered,
  Make haste therefore, to be by guilt encumbered;
  I love those amorous tricks, the wild, the mad —
  Go on, enslave me to your lust, my lad!
SECOND CITIZEN Girls, let's go, this is nothing for you!
SECOND DAUGHTER But father, we don't understand what
  any of this means!
SECOND CITIZEN Well then, if you don't understand . . . .
HERO
  This case is most obscure, without a doubt!
  Oh Duchess, how did all this come about?
DUCHESS
  You I've been searching for since searching began,
  I've never been so in love with a man,
  Multitudes of men have lain at my feet,
  Grooms, princes, authors, and armies complete,
  But ever perceiving the love of others only,
  My own stirred not a whit, leaving me lonely.
  Because there's only one man I could love on earth,
  The one who knows I am his final lover,
  Who knows what a last night 'pon my bosom's worth,
  And joys his last bloom of lust to discover.

Thus are you the handsomest man alive, today,
Made so by death, hovering about you,
Handsome too because you're lost, as they say,
By tomorrow we'll be living without you.
Why are you so somber? Why are you so still?
Go on, do with me finally what I will!
She throws herself in his arms.
HERO *after a short pause, distancing himself from her*
You've forgotten one thing, Duchess: in short,
I may not be in the mood to make sport.
SECOND CITIZEN Girls, let's go. . . .
BOTH DAUGHTERS But father, we don't understand what any
of this means!
SECOND CITIZEN But I'm embarrassed on your behalf! . . .
Let's go. . . .
DUCHESS *first looks at the hero in grand fashion, then bursts
out laughing, wildly and hysterically; suddenly she listens.*
The Duke! Where can I hide? I'm so very scared!
She escapes into the bedroom.
HERO
In what manner of destiny am I ensnared?
AUTHOR *to the Director* Now it's going fine! The scene
worked!
DIRECTOR Too late! Everything before then would've had to
have been crossed out!
AUTHOR Then they would have understood absolutely nothing!
DIRECTOR But they would have been entertained, the people!
THE SERVANT *enters*
The Duke of Lawin has come to call,
Nor has he come alone at all.
*He opens the door and lets the Duke and his escorts enter.
Then he disappears again.*

BOTH DAUGHTERS Ah! . . .

The DUKE, *dressed with fabulous elegance, enters along with the* TWO MUTE GENTLEMEN. *Mutual bows.*

DUKE
This proceeding is quite odd,
Hence I've brought two men along.
They all sit down.
I'm the Duke of Lawin, by God,
Am fiery, interesting, and strong.
In me the sap of ancient heroes flows,
My vital energy just grows and grows.
He turns to the mute gentlemen who nod in agreement.
And I can prove the truth of what I claim —
By breaking an iron bar in twain!
One of the mute gentlemen takes an iron bar from his breast pocket, hands it to the Duke who breaks it in half and throws the pieces to the floor.
And if the strongest wrestler heretofore
Appeared, I'd throw him down, his conqueror!

The WRESTLER *makes a path for himself through the audience and up to the stage. He is wearing athletic garb, with a panther skin and numerous medals. He goes up on to the marionette stage. Stirring in the auditorium.*
THE GROUCHY MAN That is really the limit!
THE NAIVE MAN I like that! Bravo, bravissimo! Now they'll go at it! *Applauds.*
AUTHOR That's just to their taste! Animals!

The Duke wrestles with the wrestler and after a brief battle throws him off the stage and among the audience. The piano player falls off his chair. Laughter.

AUTHOR Now, for God's sake, what is that!

DIRECTOR Be glad! That could save your entire comedy.

The wrestler gets up, blows kisses to the audience, and exits.

DUKE

And when I laugh, then like a shot,

The paintings fall from every spot.

He laughs in two short bursts; the paintings fall from the wall.

Out of every card I can shoot the ace!

The first mute gentleman goes to the other end of the room, hold a card in the air; the second mute gentleman hands the Duke a pistol. The Duke shoots and hits the ace. The mute gentleman shows the card to the hero.

Where I set foot, no grass grows anyplace. . . .

He steps forward; both mute gentlemen approach him and confirm that no grass is, in fact, growing there.

And never does a day go by wherein

Some little woman doesn't die for me.

A shot is fired. One of the gentlemen steps to the window, waves down; a dead girl is handed in to him through the window. He lays her on the sofa; she is holding a piece of paper in her hand; the gentleman hands the paper to the Duke; the Duke hands it to the hero without reading it.

HERO *reads*

I was in love with the Duke of Lawin,

He loved me not — now death must set me free!

At a signal from the Duke, the two gentlemen throw the body of the girl out the window.

DUKE

But for all that I am fiery and strong,

My mind is likewise noble and just,
And if ever I did any man wrong,
I acknowledge it without delay, I trust.
This, today, is my situation,
And I follow my heart's command.
Thus, to effect a reconciliation
I offer this hero my hand.

LIESL *enters.*

THE NAIVE MAN Here she is, the one who was on right at
the start.

THE GROUCHY MAN What is she doing here now!?

LIESL
The Duke!

HERO   Liesl! What is this, pray tell?
You know the Duke!

LIESL   I'm not feeling well!
She sinks down.

DUKE *about to leave.*

HERO
Not one step beyond this portal!
Duke! Do you know this sorry mortal?

DUKE
To make reply I am not obligated.

HERO
Say, Liesl, speak! — She lies annihilated!
Ha! I can imagine the connection —
This is the thanks I get for my affection!

DUKE
Since your fate you now perceive,
Let me be allowed to leave.

HERO
I'm sorry, Duke, not quite so fast. This fool

Now challenges you to a duel!
DUKE

For his own Duchess he may give dueling a whirl,
But Lawin never fights over a common girl!
Exits with the two mute gentlemen.
HERO

Here she lies, benighted, half alive,
In her unconsciousness see her languish!
Looks as if she couldn't count to five,
But how she can torture and cause anguish!
What to do now?
There is banging from the other side of the bedroom door.
The Duchess of Lawin!
Ha! I had forgotten she's still within!
Now everything's turning out marvelously well,
I'll have a rare adventure, I can tell. —
You see, Liesl, I'm no more faithful than you,
And I'll forgive you in an hour or two.
He goes to the bedroom door; the Duchess comes out.
Now let us kiss, then set the night on fire,
Now do with me whatever you desire!
DUCHESS

Please be so kind as to leave my passage free!
HERO

Oh, Duchess, just now you were in love with me!
DUCHESS

And you are?
HERO   The hero of this play!
DUCHESS

I love only him who dies the next day! *Exits.*
THE NAIVE MAN   But why? . . . why is she leaving, then?
Now she could get what's coming to her!

AUTHOR The people don't seem to be grasping this!

DIRECTOR I told you, didn't I? — It's going all wrong.

AUTHOR And the dangerous monologue is still coming!

DIRECTOR Your entire play is dangerous. It should've ended
with the wrestler.

AUTHOR How can you say that!? The wrestler occurred to us
at the last minute; he doesn't even belong there.

DIRECTOR The only good thing about your play altogether is
what doesn't belong there!

HERO

She is gone! Was it not like a reverie?

Her scent lingers, else it defies belief.

And Liesl is slumbering here so peacefully.

I ask you, what more can one add thereto?

Insofar as I grasp what I've been through,

I feel no grudge, only the slightest grief.

LIESL *opens her eyes*

Where am I?

HERO   With me.

LIESL   And the Duke?

HERO   Gone.

LIESL And I've hurt you —

HERO   That you have done.

But tell me now, how ever could you act —

LIESL It was so lovely — and that's how I am, in fact.

THE NAIVE MAN Haha! That's how she is! She is something,
that one!

HERO

Oh darling child, what if the heart break,

One can't stay mad at you, that's no mistake!

And that you were the Duke's, that too I'd love

To take as symbolic — but tell me, what of?

LIESL

You speak so smartly, you're so kind by and by!
She sinks on his bosom.

THE NAIVE MAN Now she's got him! He'll marry her yet in
the end!

THE GROUCHY MAN It's simply absurd!

THE JOVIAL MAN I don't know. . . I don't know. . . there's
something going on. . . .

HERO

Ha! — Liesl, have you the courage to die?

LIESL

Why do you ask?

HERO   In this manner alone
Can you be mine once again and atone,
And thus cleansed, at your beloved's side,
Into the bliss of eternity glide.

LIESL

No, I'd rather not.

HERO   How sweet! How obtuse!

LIESL

No, I won't kill myself — it's no use!

HERO

Then begone from my sight — you make me ill!

LIESL

What's this? Can it be? — you don't like me still?

THE SOMBER CHANCELLERY CLERK *enters.*

LIESL

Father!

SOMBER CLERK Ha! So I've found you, sad hero!
We have nothing, you have all the dough!

We slave for you and you, you violate
Our daughters while we sit home and wait!
HERO
You old man — how stale and senseless sound
Your words to one who is heaven bound!
SOMBER CLERK
To throw yourself away on this ne'er-do-well!
HERO
You needn't abuse me to take her away.

LIESL'S FIANCE *enters.*

HERO
Someone else again!
LIESL   My groom!
HERO   What the hell! —
And who might you be?
FIANCE   The lady's fiancé.
LIESL
Oh friend of my youth, patient man, is it you?
Forgive, and marry me!
FIANCE   That I will do,
I've been ready, you know, for many a year.
Have you now concluded your love's career?
LIESL
 Oh Franz, it's time, let us delay no more!
  To her father and fiancé
My place is with you, I was so blind before!
All three exit.

COMMENTATOR
Back to the routine, the job, the shop again,

Everyone returns to his place of origin.

HERO

Methinks I've lost a goodly bit —
Betrayed on all sides, and alone.
Life's not worth living, not a whit,
To my eternal rest I'll now be gone.

DEATH *enters, wearing a horrific outfit and darkly veiled.*

The citizen's wife faints.

CITIZEN Do calm down, will you?!

A flurry of activity. He leads his wife off.

AUTHOR *to the director* That's all we needed!

HERO

Who are you?

DEATH   Look at my face!

HERO   You appall me!

Away! I shudder!

FIRST SCANDALMONGER *who has sat quietly until now* Me too!

Some people laugh.

OTHERS *calling out* Shh!

DEATH   Did you not call me?

SECOND SCANDALMONGER Who was it that called him?

SEVERAL Shh!

OTHERS He's right!

AUTHOR Damn it!

DEATH I am death —

HERO   What is it you want here?

FIRST SCANDALMONGER Haha!

The second scandalmonger boos.

THE NAIVE MAN Now the fun's going to start.

THE JOVIAL MAN The people really haven't the slightest idea.

THE GROUCHY MAN Who hasn't the slightest idea? . . . Right they are. . . . One doesn't have to take everything! If I weren't so cultivated I'd want to boo also!

SEVERAL Quiet! . . . Quiet! Go on with the play!

DIRECTOR *on the steps* Ladies and gentlemen, quiet please!

SEVERAL Bravo! Bravo!

DEATH

I am death —

SECOND SCANDALMONGER But he's already said that! *Laughter.*

AUTHOR Now they're laughing, even!

DIRECTOR Now just imagine, if we hadn't given the people something to eat. . . they'd have beaten you to death a long time ago.

HERO   What is it you want here? . . .

As I already had the honor of asking you once. *Laughter.*

AUTHOR What is this! . . . This lump of garbage! No he's making fun of me.

MANY IN THE AUDIENCE Shh! Shh!

DEATH *yelling above them all*

That one there's immortal — it's you I prize!

The audience falls silent

Nor let my costume cause you any surprise,

My designer is prone to excitation.

And since the living lack all variation,

Death must appear in many a disguise.

Some people leave. — The unrest grows worse. — The grouchy man boos.

THE JOVIAL MAN And you claim to be a cultivated man?!

THE GROUCHY MAN What business is it of yours?

SEVERAL Quiet! . . . Quiet!

AUTHOR Now the people are leaving!

DIRECTOR At least those who leave can't boo.

THE JOVIAL MAN *to the grouchy one* Why don't you leave
if you don't like it?

THE GROUCHY MAN Shut your trap! *They stand up.*

SEVERAL Get out! Quiet!

The jovial man and the grouchy one sit down again.

DIRECTOR I told you: if the ending turns serious it won't help
you a bit that the beginning was a bunch of nonsense.

AUTHOR So restore some order here. . . . What's the meaning
of this? . . . What a bunch of hams!

DIRECTOR So, now you're getting fresh besides?

A number of marionettes peer out from the wings.

THE NAIVE MAN Ah, lookee here!

AUTHOR Your puppets have no discipline, get some order! Or
I will personally set this hut of yours on fire!

DIRECTOR Gentlemen!

SEVERAL Quiet! Listen!

DIRECTOR *on the steps* Gentlemen! Whenas the essence of
the Enlightenment is reflected against the background of early
history and art yields its fruit, it is then, I beg you most
humbly to envisage, that the stage, the image of earthly goings-
on, known also as mirror of the world, proposes to include
within its sphere the melancholy no less than the merry,
towards which endeavor our author, poeta vates, is also
pleasured to set sail.

MANY IN THE AUDIENCE Bravo! Bravo!

OTHERS On with the play!

DEATH *screaming*
Let author and audience both have their will
Today, and their house with laughter fill,

However, Death, in all honesty, proposes
To show its true face when the circle dance closes.
He suddenly stands there as Punch.

The COUNT OF CHAROLAIS *and* THE MASTER *enter.*

THE MASTER So, my dear Count, I think I see just enough room for the two of us.
THE COUNT OF CHAROLAIS Please — after you.
THE MASTER Oh, please, I know what's proper. You come from a five-act tragedy — I from a three-act comedy only — so, after you.
They sit down.
AUTHOR Say — for God's sake, what's this now!? *To the director* Will you take a look over here?
DIRECTOR Who are they?
THE COUNT OF CHAROLAIS Two grand gentlemen! Let whoever recognizes them salute them!
AUTHOR You ought at least to see to it that no characters from other plays take seats in your restaurant while mine is being performed.

A GENTLEMAN *who is sitting in the audience of the real theater stands up and yells out loud* This is a fraud! *The people on stage all look over, the marionettes grow uneasy, and some of them look out from the sides of the marionette theater.*

THE GENTLEMAN IN THE AUDIENCE A fraud! I won't fall for that! . . . That's not worthy of a serious theater!. . .
DIRECTOR *on the apron* My dear sir!
AUTHOR *also very near the front, wringing his hands.*

THE GENTLEMAN *going further forward* I won't let myself be cheated out of the ending! . . . *To the orchestra section* It's obvious that the author couldn't think of an ending — this quarrel was prearranged!

AUTHOR I will not tolerate this!

THE GENTLEMAN Who's talking to you! . . .

AUTHOR I am the author!

THE GENTLEMAN So what! . . . You! . . . You're no more than a part of the plot either!

AUTHOR Oho!

THE GENTLEMAN Naturally! You know very well who I mean!

DIRECTOR And you? . . . Hey! . . . Are you trying to tell me that you're a real theatergoer?

THE GENTLEMAN Oh, please!

DIRECTOR You belong up here. . . . Come on! Quickly! *He helps the gentleman get up on the stage.*

THE GROUCHY MAN But this is pure circus! *He goes down into the audience.*

THE JOVIAL MAN I don't know — something's going on here!

HERO *to Death*
Wooden sword in hand, fool's cap on your head. . . .
Alas! Is this how Death is outfitted?
Booing and stomping of feet.

THE COUNT OF CHAROLAIS
What's this —? Have I, absent-mindedly,
Wandered into the wrong century?
But no —! Not I! What drove me in now drives
Me out — where will I be when tomorrow arrives?
Exits. The marionettes all come to the front.

MARIONETTES
  Treat not us, poor folk, amiss,
  Please do not your grace withhold —
  Only the author may you scold,
  Only the author is to blame for this!
THE NAIVE MAN Is this part of the play, too?
AUTHOR *on the steps*
  The play is over! What crazy specters!
  Who'll protect me from my own characters?
  Away with you! This is quite sufficient!
  Dare not presume the theater to control!
  And if I've breathed into you enough soul
  To make you independently existent,
  Is this most saucy and irrational surge
  The thanks deserved by my creative urge?
THE MASTER *pulling the author's ear* Punch! *Exits.*
MARIONETTES
  Hey, now we can do whatever we choose!
  Talk, sing, romp about, or dance a jig!
  The decision is ours — we can't lose!
  For the audience we don't care a fig! —
  So what if the author's quite out of his mind?
  Let's begin our play, and see what we find!

At this very instant a man appears, enveloped in a blue cloak; he has a long, pale face and black hair. He carries a long bare sword in his hand. He strides as far as the steps and severs all the strings with one stroke. The marionettes collapse and lie on the floor. Amazement all around.

AUTHOR
  Who are you? Speak — before you disappear!
  You're my avenger — but what shall I call you here?

THE UNKNOWN MAN
    You ask too many questions. I don't know
    What I signify. Many an earthly day
    Have I been doomed to wander here below,
    A puzzle to me and all I meet on my way.
    This sword, however, is sure to impart
    Who had a puppet's, who merely a human heart.
    This blade severs invisible strings as well,
    As many grieving puppeteers can tell!
    He swings his sword over the entire stage; all the lights go out
    and every character except him collapses
    You too? . . . *Seeing the author collapse*
               And you? I shudder at my might!
    Is it truth I bring you, or darkest night?
    Is it heaven's. . . or hell's bidding I fulfill?
    Did Law create me — or Arbitrary Will?
    Am I a god. . . a fool. . . or the same as you?
    Am I really I — or just a symbol too?
    He comes all the way to the front
    Of course, if my sword had a looser swing,
    Could I say how some, who amid suffering
    And joy strut, boasting they are really there —
    Facing the audience
    How, for example, all of you would fare?
    He exits with a proud glance.
    As soon as he is gone the lights come on, the people stand up
    again, as do the marionettes. Military music becomes audible
    again, the author runs back and forth excitedly, the director
    climbs the steps again and begins
    Gentlemen! Here one may see the prize-winning. . . . etc.

        The curtain falls amid tremendous noise.

THE TRANSFORMATION OF PIERROT

Pantomime in One Prelude and Six Pictures

PRELUDE

A small, two-story house, with a well-tended garden, at the rear of the stage. A balcony above the main door. Next to the door, both right and left, a window. A street runs along the front of the garden, leading towards a landscape of meadows and woods on the left. Garden door to the left. Late afternoon in summer. In the garden, near the fence, a table, at which are sitting: the man of the house (Father) and his wife (Mother), their daughter, Katharina, as well as Eduard, a well-mannered and well-dressed young man. The mother is just pouring coffee. Everyone drinks. Along the street, strollers are passing by: small families, couples, individuals on outings.

THE FATHER *points up to the sky* What a beautiful day!
KATHARINA *sits still, daydreaming.*
EDUARD *turns to her lovingly, extends courtesies to her.*
KATHARINA *receives them coolly. After a while*
PIERROT *appears, wearing a fashionable summer suit. He comes down the street from the right, as a harmless stroller in good spirits. He catches sight of Katharina, appears to be*

taken with her immediately, stops, and looks at her again. She pays no attention to him. Finally he throws her a kiss.

KATHARINA *turns away angrily. The others have noticed nothing.*

PIERROT *continues on his way towards the left, turns around to look at Katharina one more time before disappearing from view.*

FATHER *rises from the table, cigar in mouth, and walks up and down in the garden in good humor. The others remain seated.*

MOTHER *very obliging towards Eduard, pours another cup of coffee for him and invites him to smoke.*

EDUARD *lights a cigarette.*

MOTHER *gets up, finally, follows the Father and gives him to understand that now would be a good time to leave the young people alone.*

FATHER *good-naturedly and cheerfully declares himself to be in agreement; he is comically tender towards his wife, with an allusion to their daughter's imminent happy married state.*

FATHER *and* MOTHER *slowly go into the house.*

EDUARD *and* KATHARINA *remain sitting by themselves at the table.*

EDUARD *ever more assiduous, but with decorum.*

KATHARINA *cool.*

It grows darker. People pass by on the street now and again.

KATHARINA *yawns.*

EDUARD *is offended, but doesn't want Katharina to notice; he continues trying to entertain her.*

KATHARINA *yawns again.*

EDUARD *gets up and, somewhat insulted, takes his leave.*

KATHARINA *extends her hand to him.*

EDUARD *kisses her hand, but is hesitant to leave.*

KATHARINA *looks at him in haughty surprise* You did say good-bye to me, didn't you?

EDUARD *the corners of his mouth twitching, withdraws. He stops at the garden gate, indicates with a movement of his hand towards the house that Katharina should deliver his compliments to her parents.*

KATHARINA *nods.*

EDUARD *exits.*

KATHARINA *alone, breathes a sigh of relief. She sits down in a rocking chair, picks up a book and reads. Strollers pass by again. Katharina follows them with her glance, especially a young couple who act as if they are very much in love. She sighs and continues with her reading, beginning to get caught up in it. Her eyes light up. She nods* Ah, what a book! Confessions of love, embraces, murderous deeds, one can read about all of them here! *Becomes absorbed in her reading again.*

PIERROT *comes past, from the left this time, and greets her courteously.*

KATHARINA *pays no attention to him.*

PIERROT *stops, greets her once again.*

KATHARINA *laughs, then goes on reading.*

PIERROT *remains standing at the fence.*

KATHARINA *acts as if she were angry, stands up, prepares to go.*

PIERROT *implores her to stay.*

KATHARINA *with a contemptuous look* What is it you want?

PIERROT I am charmed by you, permit me to join you in the garden!

KATHARINA You're mad!

PIERROT If I may not come in to you, Miss, then you come out here — do! Look what a splendid evening it is. Let's take a walk up to the meadow!

KATHARINA *withdraws in the direction of the house.*

PIERROT *reflects for a moment, then goes into the garden.*

KATHARINA *already at the entrance to the house, turns around, sees Pierrot, is astonished, makes a warding off gesture, on the point of calling out.*

PIERROT *quickly up to her* For heaven's sake, don't scream!

KATHARINA *commands him to depart at once.*

PIERROT *suddenly at her feet, takes her hand and kisses it.*

KATHARINA *becomes more confused. At his moment the Mother appears on the balcony above them and calls for Katharina.*

KATHARINA *takes fright, signals Pierrot not to move.*

MOTHER *calls for Katharina again.*

KATHARINA *comes forward, shows herself to her mother.*

MOTHER Come back into the house soon, it's getting cool. *She disappears into the room.*

KATHARINA *goes back beneath the balcony to Pierrot, pleads with him that he should finally leave.*

PIERROT No. *He pleads with her to be allowed to stay in the garden with her.* Nobody will see us there, under the tree. It's getting darker and darker, too. *He comes towards the left front with her, leading her by the hand; sits down with her at the table.*

KATHARINA *who has acted during the past few seconds as if she were powerless, resists again; nevertheless, her glance soon grows soft, indeed, tender, and she sinks down into the chair.*

PIERROT *renews his declarations of love ever more fervently.*

KATHARINA   *closes her eyes, allows herself to become intoxicated with Pierrot's words. But then, coming back to her senses, she stands up again.*

PIERROT   *wants to pull her down to himself.*

KATHARINA   Leave me alone!

PIERROT   Why are you resisting? It's not that you're unmoved, I can see it, I can feel it.

KATHARINA   *pointing to her ring*   I am engaged.

PIERROT   That doesn't bother me at all. Away with this ring.

KATHARINA   What's the idea? My parents!   *Points to the balcony.*

PIERROT   *declares himself prepared to go upstairs to the parents immediately in order to ask for Katharina's hand.*

KATHARINA   What's the idea? Who are you, really?

PIERROT   *plays the mysterious man.*

KATHARINA   If you won't tell me who you are, then go away.

PIERROT   *allows her, as if by chance, to see a handkerchief on which an eleven-pointed crown becomes visible.*

KATHARINA   *notices it.*

PIERROT   *quickly conceals the handkerchief, as if he didn't want to be discovered. The Mother suddenly appears on the balcony again, calling for Katharina.*

KATHARINA   *stands up, starts to go.*

PIERROT   When will I see you again?

KATHARINA   Never.

PIERROT   When? I implore you.

KATHARINA   *shrugs.*

PIERROT   I must see you again.

KATHARINA   *about to go.*

PIERROT   Katharina!   *Pulls her to him.*

KATHARINA   *tears herself loose and hurries into the house.*

PIERROT   *remains standing a while.*

FATHER *and* MOTHER   *appear on the balcony.*

KATHARINA   *joins them, says good night to them.*

FATHER *and* MOTHER   *kiss her on the forehead.*

PIERROT   *still in the garden, sees everything from the darkness.*

KATHARINA   *leaves the balcony.*

FATHER *and* MOTHER   *remain standing there, enjoying the mild night air. Below, a window next to the house entrance is opened.*

KATHARINA   *appears inside at the window sill.*

PIERROT   *sees her immediately, remains hidden.*

KATHARINA   *stretches out her arms, as if in longing.*

PIERROT   *creeps closer. A belated merry party comes along the street. Pierrot comes closer and closer to Katharina's window.*

KATHARINA   *sees him all of a sudden. She is startled.*

PIERROT   *signals her to remain silent, comes very close to her, takes her hand.*

KATHARINA   *asks him once again to leave, but very weakly.*

PIERROT   *after he swings himself over the window sill, one can still see him sinking at Katharina's feet.*

Then the curtain falls.

FIRST PICTURE

A small restaurant with garden in the Prater. Evening. Lanterns have been lighted. To the right a stage on which an acrobat is just performing his tricks, accompanied by a piano player. At the tables, the audience is eating and drinking. Applause. The acrobat leaves the stage.

The innkeeper, the director, the director's daughter Anna, all very excited.

INNKEEPER Where is he?

DIRECTOR I don't know.

ANNA Wherever could he be?

INNKEEPER *pointing to the audience* The people are getting impatient already.

DIRECTOR What shall I do?

CLOWN *joins the other three.*

DIRECTOR *to the clown* Get up on stage!

CLOWN *refuses.*

ANNA *pleads with him.*

CLOWN *gives in, goes up on stage, performs his antics.*

ANNA *runs to the left, as if she were hoping that the person they are waiting for would come from that direction.*

DIRECTOR *goes to the other side. Both return to the center.*

INNKEEPER *furious* You can all go to hell!

PIERROT *appears from the left, sauntering comfortably, a cigarette in his mouth, wearing the same fashionable summer suit as in the Prelude.*

ALL THREE *up to him* Where have you been keeping yourself?

ANNA *tenderly.*

DIRECTOR *urgently.*

INNKEEPER *sternly.*

DIRECTOR Now hurry up and get yourself ready and get up on stage.

PIERROT *shakes his head.*

INNKEEPER *calms the guests at the tables.*

DIRECTOR *to Pierrot* What's the big idea?

ANNA What's the matter?

DIRECTOR Hurry, hurry!

PIERROT I haven't the slightest intention. I've only come to say good-bye to you.

DIRECTOR *astonished.*

ANNA *shocked. Both throw numerous questions at him.*

PIERROT *does not answer at first, then points to a ring on his finger.*

DIRECTOR *does not understand.*

ANNA *gets an inkling of what is going on.*

PIERROT *explains more clearly, points to his heart, then again to the ring.* This is the engagement ring.

ANNA *wrings her hands in despair.*

DIRECTOR *is unable to grasp it.*

PIERROT *about to take his leave.*

ANNA *holds him back.*

DIRECTOR *calls the innkeeper to come help.*

CLOWN *and* ACROBAT *come over.*
  Everyone presses upon Pierrot.

PIERROT *shakes his head, wants to leave, they hold him back.*

DIRECTOR At least go on this one last time. You see the people are waiting.

PIERROT No. *He indicates the stage and the audience with a contemptuous gesture* Now I shall become a fine gentleman. Take a coach, ride horses, have lots of money and a house.

ANNA *cries.*

CLOWN *to Anna* Now you're crying! I told you so right away. *Some in the audience have spotted Pierrot. Two young women and their escorts come up to him, ask him why he is not performing. Others join them. All plead with him to go up on the stage.*

PIERROT *finally gives in* One more time, for the last time!
  All express their satisfaction.

PIERROT *disappears.*

ANNA *turns her back to the clown again.*

CLOWN *embittered.*

THE AUDIENCE *return to their seats.*

DIRECTOR *to the innkeeper* You see, I managed it after all.

The piano player begins a new tune.

Father, Mother, and Katharina pass by, accompanied by Eduard.

EDUARD *is speaking spiritedly to Katharina.*

KATHARINA *does not answer.*

FATHER Let's go into this inn, there's something worth seeing here.

The others agree, they enter the garden and sit down at a table.

INNKEEPER *goes over to them very courteously.*

The skit on stage begins.

The clown and Columbine (Anna). They play a love scene. The clown is importunate. Columbine resists.

KATHARINA *glances over in a cursory manner, then stares straight ahead with a blissful smile rich in memories.*

PIERROT *comes on the scene in a Pierrot costume and steps between the clown and Columbine.*

KATHARINA *is not looking over.*

EDUARD *tries in vain to draw Katharina's attention to the skit.*

PIERROT *reproaches the clown with some vehemence.*

CLOWN *replies insolently.*

PIERROT *calls him to account.*

COLUMBINE *laughs.*

PIERROT *grabs the clown by the collar, twirls him around in the air several times.*

THE AUDIENCE *charmed* Ah!

KATHARINA *casts a glance towards the stage, does not believe her eyes right away.*

PIERROT *calls the clown names, chases him and Columbine out the door. Now he stands by himself, delivers a gloomy-despairing monologue, still accompanied by the piano player.*

KATHARINA *ever more excited, stands up.*

EDUARD *calms her, without suspecting the cause of her excitement.*

THE PARENTS *to Eduard* That's just how she is. A young girl. It'll pass in time.

PIERROT *throws himself to the ground in an attack of feigned rage.*

KATHARINA *now rushes all the way up to the stage.*
When Pierrot raises his head he cannot escape looking directly into Katharina's face. He recognizes her but immediately conceals the fact that he has recognized her.

KATHARINA *stares at him.*

PIERROT *has risen, looks at her as if astonished, then immediately continues playing his scene. Walks back and forth on stage like a man in despair. Occasionally casts a sidelong glance at Katharina.*

KATHARINA *is fetched back to the table by Eduard. They all plead with her.*

MOTHER Obviously it's the play that's getting her so worked up. When I was young, I too. . . .

COLUMBINE *comes on again, goes up to Pierrot, asks his forgiveness.*

KATHARINA *stands up* Let's go, let's go!

FATHER *and* MOTHER *plead with her.*

KATHARINA No, no, away! *She gives Eduard her hand* I will marry you.

EDUARD *transported with joy.*

FATHER *pays the innkeeper.*

INNKEEPER *expresses his regret that the guests are leaving so soon. Parents, Katharina, and Eduard leave the garden.*
At this same instant, Pierrot signifies that he has hit upon a clever idea. He pushes Columbine away, as if he did not want to forgive her.
ANNA *previously Columbine, is stunned.*
PIERROT *rushes off.*
ANNA *stands there, helpless.*
The director, the clown and the acrobat come on stage, look at one another.
THE AUDIENCE *applauds.*

Scene Change

SECOND PICTURE

Another part of the Prater's amusement area. All manner of booths all around. Noise, performing bands, many people. A swing-attendant, in the process of swinging a number of house-maids and soldiers. Father, Mother, Katharina, and Eduard appear.

KATHARINA *now distracted, now purposely merry.*
EDUARD *in happy spirits.*
MOTHER Where would you like to go? To the carousel there, or to that booth over there, where the barker is yelling? Or to the circus?
KATHARINA No, no place.
FATHER *calls the swing to their attention* That's fun, to fly back and forth in the air like that!

EDUARD *elegant, is not very much in favor.*
FATHER and MOTHER *try to convince them both* Why not?
SWING-ATTENDANT *invites them courteously. They finally decide, and all four get into the swing. The attendant puts the swing in motion.*
KATHARINA *cheers up somewhat.*
MOTHER *grows afraid.*
FATHER *makes fun of her.*
EDUARD *loses his top hat.*
STREET URCHINS *below, toss it in the air.*
EDUARD *catches it.*
PIERROT *has appeared in the meantime, wearing his summer suit, presses some money into the swing-attendant's hand, partly exchanges clothes with him. The attendant puts on Pierrot's jacket, Pierrot the swing-attendant's flashy vest and his little hat which he sets jauntily on his head. He sends the swing-attendant off and takes over his duties.*
  The swing comes to a stop.
MOTHER *and* FATHER *get off first.*
KATHARINA *follows them. She sees Pierrot, starts in fright.*
PIERROT *looks her in the face with complete innocence.*
KATHARINA *looks at Pierrot's changed costume, cannot figure things out.*
EDUARD *behind her, still in the swing, urges her to get off.*
KATHARINA *gets off.*
EDUARD *likewise.*
PIERROT *walks up and down, entirely in his new role, invites other guests to step into the swing.*
KATHARINA *turns towards him.*
  New guests have gotten on.
PIERROT *begins to swing them back and forth.*

FATHER, MOTHER, KATHARINA, EDUARD   *walk past individual booths, finally entering one bearing the inscription "Photography Booth."*
PIERROT   *has observed everything; he gives the swing one last push and departs hurriedly.*
The occupants of the swing, fearful, scream for help.

Scene Change

THIRD PICTURE

The interior of a photography booth.

THE PHOTOGRAPHER   *is busy taking a couple's picture. Sitting in a chair is a cook; next to her, his hand on her shoulder, stands a corporal. The camera is standing very near the rear entrance to the booth.*
THE PHOTOGRAPHER   *is arranging the pose. The couple behave in an awkwardly funny manner. The photographer, behind the camera, takes the picture and goes into the darkroom.*
THE CORPORAL *and* THE COOK   *remain motionless in their pose.*
TWO YOUNG PEOPLE,   *artists, with long hair and flying scarves, come in.*
CORPORAL *and* COOK   *remain motionless.*
THE ARTISTS   *plant themselves in front of them.*
CORPORAL *and* COOK   *remain motionless.*
ONE ARTIST   *tickles the cook's nose with a feather.*
COOK   *remains motionless.*

CORPORAL *becomes flushed.*

PHOTOGRAPHER *reappears with the finished photograph. To the artists* What is it you want, gentlemen? *He tells the cook and the corporal that they may move and hands them the photograph.*

CORPORAL *and* COOK *extremely delighted. They exit.*

THE ARTISTS Please, we want to have our picture taken.

PHOTOGRAPHER First you pay! I know all about guys like you!

FIRST ARTIST *to the other* What do you say to this fellow? First you take the picture!

PHOTOGRAPHER No.

THE ARTISTS *strike their poses, more or less as the corporal and cook did earlier.*

PHOTOGRAPHER *furious, wants to throw them out; the two do not move.*

FATHER, MOTHER, KATHARINA, EDUARD *enter.*

PHOTOGRAPHER *welcomes them obsequiously.*

THE ARTISTS *do not stir.*

PHOTOGRAPHER *to the artists* If you'll be kind enough to leave, there are customers here.

THE FIRST ARTIST *notices Katharina, indicates he is awed by her beauty, calls her to the attention of the other artist, both abandon their pose.*

THE FIRST ARTIST *bows to Katharina.*

EDUARD *indignant, wants to put him in his place.*

THE SECOND ARTIST *pays his respects to the parents.*

PHOTOGRAPHER *offers seats.*

THE ARTISTS *place themselves in a corner of the establishment.*

PHOTOGRAPHER *brings a bench and a boulder over and arranges a picturesque group.*

THE ARTISTS *as if wanting to improve the scene, continuously interfere. At last the scene is arranged.*

MOTHER *reposes at the foot of the boulder.*

FATHER *leans picturesquely with his elbow on the peak of the boulder.*

KATHARINA *sits on the bench.*

EDUARD *stands behind her, with a look of infatuation.*

PHOTOGRAPHER *goes behind the camera and disappears under the black cloth.*

PIERROT *comes in from the back entrance, sneaks up to the photographer, grabs him and flings him into the darkroom, which he locks; he remains in his place behind the camera for a while, then comes forward with the plate and steps up to the others.*

KATHARINA *looks at him, seems downright turned to stone.*

PIERROT *as photographer* I'll be right back. *Goes into the darkroom.*

KATHARINA *paces back and forth in the booth, puts her hands to her head. To her mother* Didn't you notice? The Pierrot and the swing-attendant and this photographer, wasn't it always the same face?

MOTHER *knows nothing about it.*

FATHER *has maintained his pose.*

PHOTOGRAPHER *comes out of the darkroom, rubbing his hands; he is holding a banknote which he has just received from Pierrot.*

MOTHER *to Katharina* Here he comes now. You can see it's a completely different person.

PHOTOGRAPHER *goes back into the darkroom.*

KATHARINA *shakes her head, unable to understand.*

FATHER *has fallen asleep at the boulder.*

THE ARTISTS *remove a lance and a helmet from the wall, stick the helmet on the father's head, put the lance in his hand, and leave.*

MOTHER *turns around, takes fright at the sight of her husband.*

FATHER *wakes up.*

PHOTOGRAPHER *comes from the darkroom and brings the photograph.*

FATHER, MOTHER, KATHARINA *and* EDUARD *exit.*

Scene Change

FOURTH PICTURE

The gloomy interior of a booth, furnished so as to give it a mystical appearance. The fortune teller, wearing a magical robe, is sitting at a small table. In front of him, two young ladies and a lieutenant.

FORTUNE TELLER *is in the process of reading the palm of one of the young ladies.*

THE YOUNG LADY *is very pleased with the prophecy she has received.*

HER COMPANION *teases her.*

THE LIEUTENANT *is urged by the ladies to have his fortune told. He refuses at first, then gives in. The fortune teller imparts bad things to him. The lieutenant, offended, stands up, exits with the two ladies.*

THE CASHIER *a corpulent old woman, informs the fortune teller from outside the booth that no further customers are coming at the moment and brings him coffee.*

FORTUNE TELLER *breathes a sigh of relief, removes his white beard and his long white hair and begins to drink his coffee.*

PIERROT *comes in quickly from the rear, up to the fortune teller, and speaks to him with some urgency: he wants the beard, the hair, the robe* Here's money.

FORTUNE TELLER *stands up, removes his robe.*

PIERROT *puts it on. Likewise the white beard and the white hair. He takes the fortune teller's seat.*

FORTUNE TELLER *disappears with his coffee.*

FATHER, MOTHER, KATHARINA *and* EDUARD *enter.*

FATHER *tries to persuade Mother to have her fortune told.*

MOTHER *sits down.*

PIERROT *takes her hand, mumbles all sorts of things without raising his head.*

MOTHER *is very satisfied.*

KATHARINA *sits down. Quite absent-minded, she doesn't pay any particular attention to the fortune teller.*

FATHER *lights a cigar. He has colored matches. The room suddenly becomes very bright.*

PIERROT *raises his head.*

KATHARINA *recognizes Pierrot's eyes. Stares at him fixedly. She tears her hand abruptly from his and rushes out. The booth immediately gets dark again.*

EDUARD *goes up to Pierrot* What did you say to her?

PIERROT *shrugs.*

FATHER *and* MOTHER *have immediately gone after Katharina.*

EDUARD *rushes out into the darkness.*

PIERROT *throws off robe and beard and rushes off.*

Scene Change

FIFTH PICTURE

Another part of the Prater. All sorts of booths. An open shooting gallery close to the front. Behind the counter, young women loading the rifles. Guests shooting. In front of the counter, a punching dummy on whom someone is just testing his strength.

FATHER, MOTHER, KATHARINA *enter.*

KATHARINA *bewildered.*

MOTHER *attempts to calm her.*

KATHARINA *points to the bicycle racetrack, where she wants to go.*

MOTHER What can you be thinking of, my child?!

KATHARINA *starts to go into a different booth, is held back. Finally they arrive at the shooting gallery.*

FATHER Now I want to show you what an excellent marksman I am! *He takes a rifle, aims, and misses; this is repeated several times; the others laugh at him.*

FATHER *urging his daughter* You try it. *She is given a rifle.*

KATHARINA *aims at the eagle, then at a glass ball, hits her target both times. She receives compliments from all sides, cheers up. With her third shot she aims at the drummer. She hits her target again, he begins to drum, but suddenly, instead of his own face, the face of Pierrot has appeared.*

KATHARINA *shrieks.*

EDUARD *furious, limps in only at this moment and just sees Katharina rushing off like a madwoman.*

THE OTHERS *not understanding, stand there, helpless.*
  A great deal of confusion.
FATHER, MOTHER, EDUARD *follow after Katharina.*

Scene Change

SIXTH PICTURE

The Prater meadows along the Danube. Moonlight. At first, silence. The stage is empty. Finally Katharina rushes in. Quite disheveled, as if mad. She hurries here and there, not knowing where she is. She imagines she has killed Pierrot. Then she remembers that this is impossible. She calls the events of the evening back to mind.

KATHARINA The Pierrot in the comedy, the swing-attendant, the photographer, the fortune teller, the drummer, it was always him! But he couldn't have been everywhere, could he? . . . I am mad! I can't go on living. . . . *She hurries towards the riverbank as if intending to throw herself in the water.*
PIERROT *appears at this instant, in his summer suit, and holds Katharina back.*
KATHARINA *recognizes him, is terrified, and wants to flee.*
PIERROT *holds her fast* What is the matter with you?
KATHARINA Is it you? Really you?
PIERROT Of course.
KATHARINA How do you happen to be here?
PIERROT I've been strolling here in the moonlight, thinking of you.
KATHARINA Weren't you there, there, there?
PIERROT *acts as if he didn't understand her at all.*

KATHARINA I did see you with my own eyes. As Pierrot in the comedy, as swing-attendant, as photographer, as fortune teller, as drummer — I shot you, didn't I? —

PIERROT You're dreaming. *He acts pensive.* Ah, I'm beginning to understand. You saw me everywhere — thought you saw me everywhere — because you love me. It's exactly the same for me! I see you everywhere too. Because I love you too. . . I adore you. . . .

KATHARINA *is skeptical, would like to believe him.*

FATHER, MOTHER *and* EDUARD *enter.*

MOTHER Here she is now.

FATHER What's happened here? Who is this gentleman?

PIERROT *relates* I was taking a walk here and just happened by as this young lady was about to throw herself in the water.

MOTHER Is it true?

KATHARINA Yes, it's true.

MOTHER So he saved you!

FATHER *shakes Pierrot's hand.*

MOTHER *does likewise.*

EDUARD *stands by somberly.*

ANNA *appears, with the acrobat and the clown. She catches sight of Pierrot* There he is! *Comes up to him* Now I've got you again, you miserable creature!

KATHARINA *looks at Anna, recognizes her, recognizes the Harlequin and the clown, begins to sense the connection among them without yet wanting to believe it.*

ANNA This is Pierrot, my fiancé.

FATHER, MOTHER, EDUARD *most astonished.*

DIRECTOR *comes in, out of breath, Pierrot's Pierrot costume in his hands.* Here he is, finally!

KATHARINA *understanding everything now* So, I was not mistaken then. You are Pierrot, whom I saw playing comedy

in the inn over there, and it is among these people you
belong.

FATHER *and* MOTHER *look at one another.*

*They are joined by the swing-attendant, the photographer, the
fortune teller, and the owner of the shooting gallery with the
figure of the drummer, whose shot off head he is holding in
one of his hands.*

PIERROT *shrugs; he begins to realize that the game is lost.*

EDUARD *steps up to Pierrot, demands an explanation from
him.*

PIERROT *laughs scornfully. Then he turns to Anna* Surely you
won't be angry with me?

They all surround him, wanting an explanation.

PIERROT *causes them all to fall silent by means of an imperi-
ous movement with his hand. Merry music is heard coming
from the Prater. Pierrot invites his crowd to return with him
to the Prater, where he will treat them all in celebration of
his engagement to Anna.*

ANNA *lost in bliss.*

The others signify their approval.

*Meanwhile, the group consisting of Father, Mother, Katha-
rina, and Eduard stand somewhat at a distance from the
others.*

KATHARINA *stares fixedly at the proceedings.*

EDUARD *speaks to her.*

MOTHER Do leave her alone, you see how upset the child is.

FATHER I don't understand a thing about this entire business.

PIERROT *offers Anna his arm.*

KATHARINA *smiles bitterly, turns to Eduard and offers him
her hand.*

THE PARENTS *are amazed.*

EDUARD *cannot believe it.*

KATHARINA You may well believe it, everything is fine again, I'm your bride.

MOTHER So give her your arm, why don't you?

EDUARD *does so, but for the time being without any peace of mind — and both groups turn to leave at the same time. Pierrot's group go to the right, Katharina's to the left. After a few steps, both Katharina and Pierrot turn around, as if involuntarily. Their glances meet for a second, at first still full of memory, in tenderness and bitterness — then as strangers, in final farewell.*

They turn away from one another, and both groups proceed on their way. The music from the Prater sounds livelier. Before all the characters have left the stage, the curtain falls.

THE VEIL OF PIERRETTE

Pantomime in Three Pictures

CHARACTERS

PIERROT
PIERRETTE
PIERRETTE'S FATHER
PIERRETTE'S MOTHER
ARLECCHINO, *Pierrette's fiancé*
FRED AND FLORESTAN, *Pierrot's friends*
ANNETTE
ALUMETTE
GIGOLO, *a young man*
A FAT PIANO PLAYER
A SECOND PIANO PLAYER
A VIOLIN PLAYER
A CLARINETIST
PIERROT'S SERVANT
ELDERLY LADIES AND GENTLEMEN
YOUNG LADIES AND GENTLEMEN,
　　　wedding guests

*Time and place of the action: Vienna at the beginning of the
nineteenth century.*

FIRST PICTURE

*Pierrot's room. Modestly furnished. A desk slightly to the right
of center. In front of it an armchair. At the rear right, a sofa.
Farther forward, along the wall, a spinet with candelabra, then
an étagère containing books. Pictures on the wall above it. At
the front right, the door. At the front left, a mirror on the wall,
beneath it a chest with two candelabras and a small, empty vase.
At the left rear, a cupboard. In front of it, a small table, sofa,
two chairs and, further right, the portrait of Pierrette on an
easel. In the background, an alcove-like extension with a large
window. Panorama of the defensive walls and towers of the city.
Near the door, a clothes peg with Pierrot's hat and coat. Dusk.*

First Scene

PIERROT *(Costume: a combination of the traditional Pierrot
costume and the costume of old Vienna) is sitting at the desk,
his head propped up by both hands. He stands up, walks back
and forth in the room, and stops in front of the easel. He
implores Pierrette's portrait, threatens it, walks away from it
grudgingly, turns back, sinks to the ground before it and
sobs. He gets up, goes to the desk, opens a drawer, takes out
dried flowers, letters, ribbons, strews them all about the
desktop, rummages through them. He goes to the window,
opens it, and remains standing there a while. Sinks down onto
the sofa to the right of the window and remains there
stretched out lengthwise.*

Second Scene

It has become almost completely dark. The door to the right is opened and a fairly wide beam of light from the anteroom falls across the floor.

THE SERVANT *appears at the door. With a movement of his hand, he invites Pierrot's friends to come in.*

FRED, FLORESTAN, ANNETTE, ALUMETTE *enter.*

Behind them, a small, fat piano player.

FRED, FLORESTAN *ask the servant where his master is.*

ANNETTE, ALUMETTE *look around the room with curiosity.*

THE SERVANT *points to the chair in front of the desk* My master was sitting here.*

FRED, FLORESTAN But you can see he's not here. Bring a light, won't you?

THE SERVANT *brings a candelabra with lit candles from the anteroom and goes towards the desk.*

FRED, FLORESTAN *follow him.*

ALUMETTE *puts out the candle.*

FLORESTAN *reprimands her.*

SERVANT *lights it again. At the desk* He was sitting here.

ALL FIVE *with the servant holding the candelabra leading the way, make a circuit around the room, arriving finally at the sofa on which they discover Pierrot.*

FRED I'm going to give him a shake.

FLORESTAN *holding him back, to the servant* What's going on with your master anyway?

---

* It goes without saying that even those passages presented as dialogue in the text are to be expressed in pantomime (A.S.).

SERVANT *shrugs.*

FRED *has an idea, calls Florestan's attention to the easel with Pierrette's portrait.*

FLORESTAN *understands.*

ANNETTE, ALUMETTE *stand in front of the sofa, obviously taken with Pierrot.*

FRED, FLORESTAN *have lit a second light and are standing in front of Pierrette's portrait.*

ALUMETTE *to* ANNETTE I'm going to wake Pierrot up. *She makes as if to pull his hair.*

ANNETTE *restrains her.*

ALUMETTE *bends down, makes as if to kiss Pierrot.*

ANNETTE *restrains her.*

FRED, FLORESTAN *step away from the portrait, to where the two young women are standing.*

FRED *signals the fat piano player to sit down and play.*

THE FAT PIANO PLAYER *has been standing by the door all this time, smiling absent-mindedly.*

PIERROT *is still lying on the sofa, motionless.*

FRED, FLORESTAN *send the servant out.*

SERVANT *exits.*

Third Scene

THE FAT PIANO PLAYER *has sat down at the spinet and begins to play a waltz.*

FLORESTAN, ALUMETTE *and* FRED, ANNETTE *dance with one another.*

PIERROT *wakes up. Looks around. Doesn't understand what has taken place, rubs his eyes. Jumps up, comes forward.*

THE TWO COUPLES *don't let him interfere with their dancing.*

FLORESTAN *and* ALUMETTE *finally sink down onto the small sofa on the left, alongside the little table.*

FRED *and* ANNETTE *remain standing next to the spinet.*

PIERROT *is leaning against the desk.*

FRED, FLORESTAN, ANNETTE, ALUMETTE *look at him and laugh. They go up to him in couples and bow.*

FRED, FLORESTAN *introduce their respective ladies.*

ANNETTE, ALUMETTE *curtsy gracefully.*

PIERROT *makes a deep bow.*

FRED A fine state we've found you in. What has happened to you?

PIERROT Don't ask me.

FLORESTAN *cordially* Do tell us what's the matter, maybe we can help you.

PIERROT Never mind. I'm beyond help.

FRED I can imagine it has to do with Pierrette.

PIERROT Leave me alone, won't you?

ANNETTE, ALUMETTE *hurry over to the portrait, as if they intended removing it from the easel.*

PIERROT *follows them, walks up to them, then shields the portrait by standing in front of it, arms outspread.*

FRED He's crazy. There's nothing to be done with him.

FLORESTAN *takes hold of Pierrot's hands, slowly moves him away from the picture, leads him over to the desk.*

FRED Put this business out of your mind, Pierrot, it's not worth the effort to worry about Pierrette. Come with us.

FLORESTAN Yes, come with us.

ANNETTE, ALUMETTE *press themselves on Pierrot.* Come with us.

PIERROT *frees himself from the others with a gesture of disgust. Sits down in the chair at the desk.*

FRED, FLORESTAN *still trying to persuade him* Come with us. Let's have a good time. It's a lovely evening. Let's go outdoors. Let's drink, dance, kiss.

PIERROT *remains seated and shakes his head.*

FRED, FLORESTAN *become more pressing.*

ANNETTE, ALUMETTE *join in, pleading and cajoling.*

FRED, FLORESTAN, ANNETTE, ALUMETTE *close a circle around Pierrot and dance around him.*

THE FAT PIANO PLAYER *accompanies them on the spinet.*

PIERROT *stands up. Angrily* Leave me in peace. I can't stand it any longer. I can't listen to this playing. Go.
Hurries to the spinet, violently bangs it shut. He goes to the window at the rear.

THE FAT PIANO PLAYER *has started in fright.*

FRED, FLORESTAN, ANNETTE, ALUMETTE *look at each other questioningly, thoughtfully, angrily.*

FLORESTAN Let's leave him alone.

FRED The hell with him.

ANNETTE, ALUMETTE What a pity.

PIERROT *stands at the window with folded arms.*

THE TWO COUPLES *bow to him ironically and dance out of the room.*

THE FAT PIANO PLAYER *follows them.*

Fourth Scene

PIERROT *at the window, looks out apathetically.*

SERVANT *enters.*

PIERROT *does not notice him right away.*

SERVANT *draws nearer.*

PIERROT *takes a few steps towards him* What do you want?

SERVANT Kind sir, I would like the evening off.

PIERROT What for?

SERVANT I'm in love and long to be together with my beloved.

PIERROT *turns away in disgust.*

SERVANT *remains standing where he is, waiting in vain for a reply. Approaches Pierrot pleadingly once more.*

PIERROT *turns back to him* Go wherever you like.

SERVANT *thanks him emphatically.*

PIERROT *impatiently* Just go, just go already.

Fifth Scene

PIERROT *alone. He goes to the desk, throws the flowers and letters to the floor. Paces back and forth.*
He takes his hat and coat from the peg.
I want to go away, it doesn't matter where. Into the open, to solitude, perhaps to death.
He goes to the window, looks down. Suddenly he becomes attentive. Leans far out over the window-sill. Starts back.
Is it possible? No, I'm dreaming.
Leans out again, clearly following a figure moving along the wall of his house, beneath his window. He leans out still further. The figure seems to have entered the building and to have vanished from his view. He steps away from the window back to the middle of the room in doubtful astonishment. He listens. There can be no further doubt, steps are to be heard on the staircase. He rushes into the anteroom and disappears.

Sixth Scene

PIERROT   *still in his coat, but not wearing his hat, enters the room with Pierrette, whom he holds by both hands, the greatest astonishment in his features.*

PIERRETTE   *(in an old-Vienna wedding dress with nuances of a Pierrot costume. A garland of myrtle. A veil about her head and shoulders) stands there as if paralyzed, looks at Pierrot with a blissful-distracted glance.*

PIERROT   Am I dreaming? Am I awake? Is it you? Is it me? How is it possible that you're here?

PIERRETTE   *moving her head softly* Just let me come to my senses. Yes, I'm here. With you. *She begins to totter.*

PIERROT   *supports her with his arms, leads her over to a chair, front left, next to the little table.*

PIERRETTE   *sinks into the chair.*

PIERROT   *falls to his knees in front of Pierrette, covers her hands with kisses* Now everything is all right again, since I have you. But now, at last, explain to me . . . .

PIERRETTE   *looks at him with mute eyes.*

PIERROT   *stands up, flings the coat aside* So tell me. I beg of you. Where are you coming from? I don't understand a thing that's going on.

PIERRETTE   *remains silent. Looks fearfully in the direction of the window, as if she had heard a sound.*

PIERROT   *calms her, hurries to the window, looks down, closes it. Hurries to the door, looks into the anteroom, locks the door. Hurries back to Pierrette.*

PIERRETTE   *who has stood up, spreads her arms to Pierrot.*

PIERROT   *falls back from her, points to her myrtle garland and her veil* Explain to me. Tell me, finally.

PIERRETTE *spreading her arms* Come.
The veil slides down off her shoulders and remains lying on the floor at the front.

PIERROT No, I'm afraid. Where are you coming from?

PIERRETTE What do you care about that now? You see I'm here with you.

PIERROT *points to the window and beyond* But what has happened with you out there in the world in the meantime?

PIERRETTE Don't ask. That's over, now I'm with you and I will stay with you. *She pulls a small silver vial out of her belt* Look what I've brought.

PIERROT What is that?

PIERRETTE This is poison. Let us die together.

PIERROT *takes the vial from her hand* What? We're supposed to drink this?

PIERRETTE Yes.

PIERROT Why should we die? Come, let us run away, rather.

PIERRETTE *shakes her head.*

PIERROT *leads her over to the window* But look how beautiful the world is. It's all ours. Come, let's run away.

PIERRETTE Run away? No! Where to? What shall we do? We have no money. There is no other way, we have to die.

PIERROT *shakes his head.*

PIERRETTE If you don't want to, then I'll leave you here and go away again. Farewell. *She turns to go.*

PIERROT Stay, stay.

PIERRETTE What for?

PIERROT In order to. . . . We will drink the poison and die together. *He puts his arm around her and goes with her to the sofa on the left.*

PIERROT *and* PIERRETTE *sit down.*

PIERROT   *embraces Pierrette passionately then stands up abruptly.*

PIERRETTE   *remains seated and looks at him with wide open eyes.*

PIERROT   *goes to the cupboard at the rear left, opens it, takes out two bottles of wine and several glasses. He brings everything forward and places it on the table.*

PIERRETTE   *stands up also, goes to the cupboard, takes from it pastry, fruit, a tablecloth, plates, and silverware. She hastily sets the table.*

PIERROT   *helps her.*

BOTH   *act with forced gaiety.*

PIERRETTE   *takes flowers from her belt, hurries over to the chest, puts the flowers in the small vase, brings it over and places it on the table.*

PIERROT *and* PIERRETTE   *hop arm in arm through the room, lighting it up festively. They light the candles on the desk, on the chest, on the spinet.*

PIERROT   *with playful dignity, offers Pierrette his arm and leads her to the table.*

BOTH   *sit down on the sofa, eat and drink.*

PIERROT   *moves closer to Pierrette.*

PIERRETTE   *nestles against Pierrot. Long embrace.*

PIERROT   *suddenly standing up* It is time —

PIERRETTE   *shudders.*

PIERROT   *takes the vial and pours half its contents in each of the still half-filled wine glasses. He lifts his glass, asks Pierrette to clink glasses.*

PIERROT *and* PIERRETTE   *clink glasses.*

PIERRETTE   *puts her glass down.*

PIERROT   *does likewise.*

PIERRETTE   *walks slowly to the rear.*

PIERROT *follows her.*

   Near the window they embrace once more.

BOTH *arms still around one another, slowly return to the table.*

PIERROT Are you ready?

PIERRETTE Yes.

PIERROT *picks up his glass.*

PIERRETTE *hesitates.*

PIERROT *smiles scornfully* You don't have the courage after all. You see, I thought as much.

PIERRETTE Oh, Pierrot, don't you believe that. I have the courage. Just one more kiss, then I'll be ready.

BOTH *embrace one another passionately. They put the glasses to their lips and look into each other's eyes a long time. They both incline their heads back.*

PIERROT *empties his glass at one draught.*

PIERRETTE *has not managed to drink a single drop.*

PIERROT *noticing this, staggers back in shock.*

PIERRETTE *having moved the glass away from her mouth a little, now puts it back to her lips.*

PIERROT *scornfully knocks the glass out of her hand. Sinks lengthwise to the floor behind the easel (in such a way that he would not be seen at once by a person entering the room).*

PIERRETTE *stands there transfixed. She then throws herself down before Pierrot, grabs hold of him. shakes him, kisses him. All in vain. She picks up the glass, shows it to Pierrot* Just look here, I do want to do it. *She puts the glass to her lips, notices it is empty, and shatters it. She stands up, runs back and forth in the room grasping her head helplessly, feels the myrtle garland, and winces. Suddenly she thinks she has heard a sound, hurries to the window, cowers on the sofa. She comes to the front again, to Pierrot; looks down at him in fear.* You're alive, right, you're alive? Answer me,

Pierrot! *She bends over him, lower and lower, looks at him with increasing terror until she finally grasps that he is dead. Horrified, she runs to the door, flings it open, and rushes off.*

Curtain

The music leads into the second picture without pause.

SECOND PICTURE

A banquet hall. In the background an extensive suite of rooms which, seen from the front, ascends slightly. Festive lighting. A buffet at the rear left of the front hall. To the right, a piano and music stands. Spiral staircases left and right going up to the second hall.

First Scene

A WEDDING PARTY
A NUMBER OF COUPLES *dancing a waltz.*
OLDER LADIES AND GENTLEMEN *sitting along the walls.*
TWO SERVANTS *behind the buffet, occupied with pouring wine for the guests and serving pastry.*
PIANO PLAYER, VIOLIN PLAYER, CLARINETIST *are providing the music for dancing.*
PIERRETTE'S FATHER and MOTHER *(small, cozy people) are standing at the buffet complimenting the guests.*
ARLECCHINO *(Pierrette's fiancé, tall, lean, no longer young, in an entirely black old-Vienna costume with a large white*

flower in his lapel) somber and irritated, is standing front right with folded arms, watching the dancers.

The waltz ends.

THE COUPLES *stroll about the hall.*

FATHER *and* MOTHER *come to the center of the hall.*

YOUNG GENTLEMEN *speak with the mother.*

YOUNG LADIES *speak with the father.*

GIGOLO *the dance master, very young, dressed with exaggerated elegance, scurries back and forth in the hall, now at the buffet, now by the musicians, now with individual dancers.*

SOME OF THE COUPLES *go to the buffet.*

FATHER *in good spirits, escorts two young ladies to the buffet.*

TWO YOUNG GIRLS *go up to Arlecchino and speak to him, smiling.*

ARLECCHINO'S *face remains somber.*

SEVERAL GUESTS *clink glasses with Father and Mother.*

FATHER *goes up to Arlecchino with two full glasses, hands him one. He clinks glasses with him and embraces him.*

THE PEOPLE STANDING NEAR THEM *express their approval (not by clapping hands).*

GIGOLO *claps hands, encourages the gentlemen to ask the ladies to dance, goes busily back and forth.*

THE COUPLES *prepare to dance a quadrille.*

GIGOLO *to Arlecchino* You must join in the dance too, Herr Arlecchino, do ask your bride, won't you?

ARLECCHINO *nods seriously, looks around the hall. The quadrille begins.*

GIGOLO *notices that Arlecchino is still alone, orders the music to stop.*

ARLECCHINO *to Gigolo* As you can see, Miss Pierrette is not here yet. I'm sure she's upstairs in her room. Just go on with the quadrille.

GIGOLO By no means, that won't do. *He hurries over to the mother* Herr Arlecchino is without a partner, Miss Pierrette is not here.

MOTHER *astonished, looks around the hall* Pierrette is not here? Oh yes, I know, she's in her room, getting dressed, getting ready for the trip.

FATHER *has joined them* Go up and get her, why don't you?

MOTHER *exits quickly, to the right.*

GIGOLO *gives the musicians a signal.*

THE MUSICIANS *play a minuet. The couples previously prepared for the quadrille dance the minuet.*

ARLECCHINO *in the meantime, goes to the far rear of the suite of rooms at the back, where he paces back and forth.*

MOTHER *returns, goes quickly up to the father. Pulls him forward* Pierrette is not upstairs.

FATHER You're crazy.

MOTHER I assure you, she is not upstairs.

FATHER But how is that possible?

ARLECCHINO *is suddenly standing next to them* Where is Pierrette?

MOTHER *embarrassed* She'll be here right away.

ARLECCHINO Where is Pierrette?

MOTHER *confused* I don't know.

ARLECCHINO *takes hold of the mother's arm.*

FATHER *tries to stop him.*

ARLECCHINO *stamps on the floor* Where is Pierrette?

THE COUPLES *have noticed there is something going on.*

THE DANCE MUSIC *stops.*

ONE COUPLE *standing next to the group composed of Arlecchino, Father and Mother becomes aware of what the matter is, tells the couple next to them.*

THE SECOND COUPLE *tells the others.*

The excitement is great, they all surround Arlecchino, Father and Mother, who are now standing in the center of the hall.

ARLECCHINO *threatening* I will exact terrible vengeance. I will set the house on fire. I will kill everyone.

GIGOLO *approaches* Surely the house has not been thoroughly searched yet. *To the young women* Search, all of you, do search everywhere.

THE YOUNG WOMEN *go off in all directions, some up the staircases, and run back and forth.*

THE YOUNG GENTLEMEN *stand together in groups.*

ARLECCHINO *at the front, paces back and forth with great strides.*

FATHER *and* MOTHER *on the right, fairly far back, reproach each other.*

THE YOUNG WOMEN *return little by little* We have not found Pierrette.

ARLECCHINO *becomes enraged. Goes to the buffet, smashes several glasses and bottles. Makes threatening gestures at Father and Mother. Goes over to the piano, smashes the keys, tears the violin and clarinet out of the musicians' hands, shatters them and throws them to the floor. Then he rushes to the rear, through the suite of rooms.*

Second Scene

As soon as Arlecchino reaches the rear, he is met by Pierrette.

ARLECCHINO *grabs Pierrette by the hand, pulls her forward and stops in the center.*

THE OTHERS *astonished.*

SEVERAL *seek to come closer.*

ARLECCHINO *commands them to keep their distance.*

ARLECCHINO *and* PIERRETTE *in the center of the hall.*

THE OTHERS *at a measured distance.*

ARLECCHINO *to Pierrette* Where have you been?

PIERRETTE Upstairs in my room.

ARLECCHINO That's not true.

PIERRETTE I went for a walk, out in the garden.

ARLECCHINO We searched for you, you were not in the house and not in the garden.

PIERRETTE I can't give you any other answer. Come, I want to dance.

ARLECCHINO No, first you must answer me.

PIERRETTE I want to dance.

ARLECCHINO Answer me first!

FATHER, MOTHER, GIGOLO, YOUNG WOMEN *come closer, attempt to calm Arlecchino.*

ARLECCHINO *pays no attention to them.*

GIGOLO *gives the musicians a signal.*

THE MUSICIANS *point to their ruined instruments in despair.*

GIGOLO It doesn't matter, just play, it'll be all right.

THE MUSICIANS *begin to play a fast polka. The instruments sound dreadful.*

GIGOLO *has stepped to the center of the hall* Dance, dance.

PIERRETTE *turns to Arlecchino with a desperate Bacchic gesture. She nestles closer to him.*

ARLECCHINO *looks at her a long time, puts his arm around her, dances with her.*
  Everything appears to be in order again. All of a sudden, one can see the dead Pierrot approaching slowly from the rear; he is visible only to Pierrette.

PIERRETTE *stops dancing, points in terror to the ever-approaching Pierrot.*

THE OTHERS *do not know what the matter is with Pierrette.*

PIERROT *strides through the center of the hall, stops in front of Pierrette and dissolves into nothing.*

PIERRETTE *rejects the vision as a hallucination, recovers.*

THE OTHERS *begin to dance again.*

PIERRETTE *goes to the buffet with Arlecchino. Asks the servant for something to drink.*
Suddenly, Pierrot is standing behind the buffet in place of the servant. He pours a glass of wine for Pierrette.

PIERROT *staggers back, rushes to the piano like one pursued.*

ARLECCHINO *follows her.*
The dead Pierrot vanishes.

ARLECCHINO What is the matter? What is wrong with you?

PIERRETTE Nothing, nothing. It's passing already. *She shudders and makes as if to cover herself with her veil.*

ARLECCHINO *suddenly noticing* You miserable. . . .

THE DANCE MUSIC *stops.*

ARLECCHINO Where is your veil, Pierrette?

PIERRETTE *touches her head and shoulders.*

ARLECCHINO Where is your veil?

PIERRETTE I don't know.

ARLECCHINO You lost the veil while you were gone. Where is the veil? Where were you?

PIERRETTE Leave me alone, will you.

ARLECCHINO You must retrieve your veil.

PIERRETTE I don't know where it is.
At this moment, the dead Pierrot appears in the background with the veil in his hands and comes forward only a little way. He stops at the rear of the hall.

PIERRETTE *hurries towards the dead Pierrot.*

ARLECCHINO *follows her, grabs her by the hand.*

THE DEAD PIERROT *withdraws again with the veil.*

PIERRETTE *tries to grab the veil.*
ARLECCHINO *continues to hold her by the hand.*
PIERROT *vanishes with the veil.*
PIERRETTE *follows the apparition.*
ARLECCHINO *still with her.*
SEVERAL YOUNG GENTLEMEN *make as if to follow.*
ARLECCHINO *turns around and forbids anyone to follow.*

Curtain

The Music leads into the third picture without pause.

THIRD PICTURE

The same scene as in the first.

First Scene

PIERROT *is lying stretched out, dead, on the floor behind the easel. The veil is lying there, in the middle of the dark room, gleaming white. Most of the candles have burned down, some have gone out completely. The stage remains completely empty for a few moments. The door opens.*
ARLECCHINO *and* PIERRETTE *enter.*
ARLECCHINO *is holding Pierrette by the hand.*
PIERRETTE *hurries over to the veil, bends down, hold it up high* Here it is. Now let's go.
ARLECCHINO No. Where am I here? *He goes back and forth in the room. He is standing in front of Pierrot's body, starts back, but takes Pierrot to be not dead but drunk. He turns to*

Pierrette. So that was it? You were together with this person? *He notices the remainders of the meal* Here you ate and drank together. Here he held you in his arms. Just you wait, both of you. *Goes back to Pierrot.*

PIERRETTE *rushes up to him, wants to hold him back.*

ARLECCHINO *flings her off him.*

PIERRETTE *creeps over to the window.*

ARLECCHINO *kneeling in front of Pierrot* You scoundrel, you dog. Who are you, anyway? Answer! Answer! Get up! *He grabs Pierrot by the shoulders and shakes him.*

THE DEAD PIERROT *falls heavily back to the floor.*

ARLECCHINO *starts back, terrified. He goes over to Pierrette, who is standing motionless at the window* Did you know?

PIERRETTE Yes.

ARLECCHINO *paces back and forth in thought. Turns back to Pierrette, looks at her a long while* What shall I do with you? *He has an idea, bursts out laughing in scorn. Strides back to the dead Pierrot, is about to pick him up.*

PIERRETTE *hurries forward, horrified.*

ARLECCHINO *orders her to keep her distance, takes Pierrot's body, carries it to the sofa, leans it against the front corner.*

PIERRETTE *has crept in horror to the end of the room and observes Arlecchino's activities.*

ARLECCHINO *sits down at the table facing Pierrot. Pours two glasses of wine, raises one, drinks Pierrot's health. Then, with a diabolic smile, he beckons Pierrette over.*

PIERRETTE *remains standing, motionless.*

ARLECCHINO *stands up, beckons to Pierrette peremptorily.*

PIERRETTE *approaches slowly.*

ARLECCHINO *goes to her, offers her his arm in the center of the room, escorts her to a chair next to the table, puts one of the filled glasses in her hand, clinks glasses with her.*

PIERRETTE *is unable to drink.*

ARLECCHINO So drink.

PIERRETTE *drinks.*

ARLECCHINO *sits down next to Pierrette, presses closer to her, puts his arm around her, seeks to pull her closer to him.*

PIERRETTE *shudders.*

ARLECCHINO *becomes more tender.*

PIERRETTE *jumps up, her chair falls over, she flees to the alcove at the back.*

ARLECCHINO *follows her, acts the enamored man* I worship you, my dear. *Kneels, tries to pull her to him and with him.*

PIERRETTE *runs from him, until she comes to a stop behind the dead Pierrot at the left rear.*

ARLECCHINO *has stood up, walks up to Pierrot, bows to him, then bows to Pierrette* You are in good company, I see. *He then goes to the door.*

PIERRETTE *follows his movements with growing terror.*

ARLECCHINO *turns around once more at the door and bows scornfully.*

PIERRETTE *rushes after him, throws herself on her knees before him.*

ARLECCHINO *shakes her off, exits and locks the door behind him.*

Second Scene

PIERRETTE *makes a row at the door. Hurries to the window, flings it open. Sees Arlecchino leaving, calls him to come back. He disappears from her sight. She returns to the door, shakes, tugs, in vain. She runs around the room looking for any exit. She finds none. Finally she stops again across from the dead Pierrot. She looks at him a long while, runs away. She returns. Nods to him. Flies into a terror again, creeps back and forth along the wall through the entire room. Her movements change, becoming dance-like. Her eyes express the beginnings of madness. She is behind Pierrot again, creeps slowly behind the sofa, towards him. Half-kneeling, she looks in his face. Bows to him. Begins to dance, at first in front of him, then in ever-wider arcs, finally around the entire room. She stops, the resumes dancing again with renewed strength. A noise at the door.*

PIERRETTE *is almost out of breath, her strength begins to fade, her eyes are shining dully, she is close to expiring. Renewed, louder noise at the door.*

PIERRETTE *sinks to the floor, dead, at the feet of Pierrot. The door is broken open.*

Third Scene

FRED, FLORESTAN, ANNETTE, ALUMETTE *enter. Morning has dawned. The sun is beginning to rise.*

FRED *and* FLORESTAN *turn to the women, laughing. Both couples skip arm in arm until they are quite close to Pierrot and Pierrette, grasp what has taken place, and fall back in horror.*

Curtain

AFTERWORD

by Herbert Lederer
Professor Emeritus, University of Connecticut

In its December 1931 issue, *Theater Arts Monthly* published an obituary of Arthur Schnitzler, who had died on October 21. The unsigned article claimed that "Schnitzler did not write a single great play." This was an astonishing statement to make about an author who was one of the most prolific and most widely performed dramatists of his age. In his lifetime, he had written no fewer than nineteen full-length and thirty-one one-act plays. Between 1891 and 1931, over seventy different Schnitzler productions had been staged in Vienna alone. No statistics are available about the number of Schnitzler plays which were performed on other German-speaking stages — let alone productions in other countries, including the United States. We do know, however, that on October 14, 1911, *Das weite Land* (*"The Vast Domain"*) was premiered simultaneously in nine European cities.

In addition to being a famous playwright, Schnitzler also wrote two novels and fifty-six short fiction works. Several of them were considered sufficiently dramatic in nature to be transformed into radio plays, films, or television productions. These include an early radio version of *Leutnant Gustl* (*"Lieutenant Gus"*), the 1929 silent movie *Fräulein Else*, starring Elisabeth Bergner and the MGM sound film of 1931, "Daybreak", directed by Jacques Feyer and starring Ramon Navarro, based on the novella *Spiel im Morgengrauen* (*"Game at Dawn"*). The same story was also dramatized on German TV, as was *Leutnant Gustl* in 1963, with a script by Ernst Lothar. As recently as 1974, the BBC produced a five-part series of TV plays based on Schnitzler's stories, entitled "Vienna 1900: Games of Love and Death." These shows were also seen on American public television.

To a large extent, to be sure, Schnitzler's most famous works were those written before World War I. His plays and his fiction have often been described as a kind of "Last Waltz in Imperial Vienna," an almost clinical analysis of an old order in its death throes. Unquestionably, his early dramas were performed most frequently, and are the ones which even now are most closely associated with him. His first success, *Liebelei*, premiered in Vienna in 1895, had originally been called "*Das arme Mädel*" ("*The Poor Girl*"). It was performed in New York in 1905 under the title "Flirtations." Since then, it has also been translated, published, and produced as "Light o' Love" and "Playing with Love." As early as 1914, the play was made into a Danish silent film called "Elkovsleg," to be followed by a German silent movie in 1927. A German sound film was directed by Max Ophuls in 1931, who also made a French version in 1932. The play also was the basis of the libretto for the opera "Liebelei" by Franz Neumann, composed in 1909 and premiered in 1910 in Frankfurt am Main. Schnitzler did not live to see a 1934 operetta by Oscar Straus also (loosely) based on his play.

Another early Schnitzler success, *Anatol*, was not performed as a full-length play until 1910, when Otto Brahm directed the cycle of scenes at the Lessing Theater in Berlin, although single scenes had been staged since 1890. Only two years later, in 1912, five of the episodes were produced in English at the Little Theater in New York, with John Barrymore in the title role. The *New York Evening World* said in its review: "If you have read

Schnitzler's 'Anatol' dialogues you know how good they are, but until you go to the Little Theater you can not know how much better they act than read." The critic for the *New York Dramatic Mirror* called Anatol Barrymore's best role, "a lovable scamp who may be unmoral but never immoral." Later American productions included one in 1931 starring Joseph Schildkraut, another in 1946 directed by Mady Christians, six scenes off Broadway in 1956, and the entire seven-episode cycle in 1958, again at the Little Theater. 1961 saw the brief run of a musical based on the play entitled "The Gay Life" (at a time when the word "gay" was still innocent of present-day implications). In spite of the praise given to Barbara Cook in the role of Liesl who finally traps Anatol into marriage — the Ilona of the original version — the show had only limited success. The play's staying power was demonstrated once again in 1984 by a critically acclaimed production at the Hartford Stage Company starring and directed by Mark Lamos. Much earlier, *Anatol* had already attracted the attention of Cecil B. DeMille who in 1921 made it into a silent film called "The Affairs of Anatol."

Schnitzler's most famous — or infamous — play *Reigen* (first called "*Liebesreigen*") was written in 1896-97 and not originally intended for the stage. Although Schnitzler circulated 200 copies of the manuscript among his friends in 1910, clearly marked "Not for sale," he did not at first believe that it could ever be published, let along produced. He turned out to be wrong. The play's stage history, however, is filled with scandal. Demonstrations during the premiere at the Kleines Schauspielhaus in Berlin in 1920 led to a lengthy court trial which eventually ended with the producer's exoneration and probably enhanced the success of the play considerably. It was variously published in English translation as "Hands Around," "Couples," "Dance of Love," "Round Dance," and "Merry-Go-Round." It is most widely

known, however, by its French title "La Ronde," under which
it was filmed twice: first by Max Ophuls in 1950, starring Adolf
Wohlbrück (later Anton Walbrook), Simone Signoret, Danielle
Darrieux, and Jean-Louis Barrault, with music by Oscar Straus;
and again by Roger Vadim in 1964, with Jane Fonda and with
a screen play written by Jean Anouilh. It was as "La Ronde" that
the play saw its first American production in 1955 at the Circle
in the Square in New York, translated by Eric Bentley and
directed by Jose Quintero. A new translation, with the same title,
was performed in 1960 and did not meet with critical success. A
musical version called "Roundelay" with book and lyrics by
Jerry Douglas lasted only for six performances. For obvious
reasons, the play — by whatever title — has long been a favorite
of American college theater productions.

Only a few of Schnitzler's later full-length plays were
produced in the U.S. *Der einsame Weg* ("*The Lonely Way*"),
written and premiered in 1904, was shown in 1931 by the
Theater Guild at the National Theater in Washington, D.C.
Professor Bernhardi, first performed in 1912 at the Kleines
Theater in Berlin, was briefly seen in New York in 1936 in an
English version directed by the playwright's son Heinrich
Schnitzler. English translations had been published earlier, in
1913 and 1927.

The 1911 premiere of *Das weite Land* at the Vienna Burgtheater was directed by Hugo Thimig, who also played a minor
role. In 1923, it was published in an English translation as *The
Vast Domain*. I am not aware of its performance record under
that title. In 1980, however, a new English version by Tom
Stoppard, called *Undiscovered Country*, was seen on the London
stage. Its critical acclaim was repeated for the American
production at the Hartford Stage Company in 1981, again
directed by Mark Lamos. Stoppard, who does not know German,

worked from a literal translation and managed to capture the spirit of the original extremely well. His choice of title, however, was unfortunate. *Das weite Land*, referring to the human soul, carries echoes of both Goethe and Freud, allusions which are at least partly rendered by *The Vast Domain*. *Undiscovered Country*, on the other hand, is clearly a quotation from Hamlet's "To be or not to be" monologue and refers to the land of the dead — an inappropriate reference for Schnitzler's play.

None of the dramas written after World War I have ever been produced in the United States; three of them, *The Sisters, or Casanova in Spa* (*Die Schwestern oder Casanova in Spa*), *Seduction Comedy* (*Komödie der Verführung*), and *The Way to the Pond* (*Der Gang zum Weiher*), translated for the first time by G. J. Weinberger, were published by Ariadne Press in Riverside, California in 1992.

Although a number of the one-act plays have been translated into English, they have only rarely been performed. *Literatur*, premiered at the Deutsches Theater in Berlin in 1902, was first performed in New York in 1908 under the title *The Literary Sense*, and has seen a few professional and amateur productions since then. *Der grüne Kakadu* (*The Green Cockatoo*) was first produced in English at the Lyceum Theater in New York in 1910. The Pabst Theater in Milwaukee performed it in 1917 in an evening of three Schnitzler one-act plays together with *The Lady with the Dagger* and *The Farewell Supper* scene from *Anatol*. *The Green Cockatoo* returned to New York in 1930 in a Civic Repertory Theater production directed by Eve Le Gallienne, with Burgess Meredith in the small role of Grain. The play was repeatedly translated into English in 1910, 1913, 1917, 1932, and 1986. In 1932, it was included in the Samuel French catalog of *Plays for the College Theater*.

In addition to numerous English translations, Schnitzler's plays were also translated into Danish, French, Hungarian, Italian, Russian, and Japanese, and were produced in the respective countries.

In light of such unquestionable prominence in the international repertoire, it is difficult to understand the reason for the negative judgment made in the *Theater Arts Monthly* obituary. Perhaps it was a result of the frequently expressed belief that Schnitzler's works were of limited appeal since almost all of them take place in Vienna at the turn of the century. As it happens, this criticism does not apply to two of the plays in the present volume: *Paracelsus* is set in sixteenth-century Basel, and *The Green Cockatoo* takes place in Paris on the eve of the French revolution. But writing plays mainly about their own country, their own time, and their own social class hardly hurt the reputation of a Molière, an Ibsen, a Chekhov, or an Oscar Wilde — or, in the realm of prose fiction, a James Joyce.

Another criticism often raised against Schnitzler is his alleged exclusive preoccupation with the themes of love and death — witness the title of the BBC series of dramatizations mentioned above. But these are central aspects of human life and hence predominate in the works of all great dramatists, from Greek tragedy to Shakespeare to Eugene O'Neill. And they are by no means Schnitzler's exclusive concerns. Again and again he deals with such topics as free will versus determinism, the transitory nature of all human experience, the blurred boundaries between reality and illusion, the significance of dreams, the power of the mind, the impossibility of finding the ultimate meaning of existence, the basic loneliness of every person's life, and the constant role-playing in which we are engaged. These are some of the issues raised by the plays in this volume.

The two pantomimes *The Transformation of Pierrot* and *The Veil of Pierrette* appear here in English translation for the first time. Schnitzler sketched the idea for *Pierrette* as early as 1895, but laid it aside. In 1898-99 he used the motif of a woman leaving her veil behind at her lover's (reminiscent of Desdemona's handkerchief in Shakespeare's *Othello*) in a five-act play *Der Schleier der Beatrice* ("*Beatrice's Veil*"), originally entitled *Der Shawl*. In 1908, Schnitzler returned to his original plan and rewrote the pantomime as a libretto for a ballet with music by Ernst von Dohnányi. A piano score was published in 1909 and the text appeared in print in 1910. In the same year, the work was premiered at the Royal Opera House in Dresden. In 1925, Schnitzler witnessed a guest performance of *Der Schleier der Pierrette* by the Moscow Chamber Theater visiting Berlin. There is no record of subsequent performances.

Using the traditional *commedia dell' arte* figures of Pierrot, Pierrette, and Arlecchino, the play revolves around the themes of love, betrayal, and revenge which occur frequently in Schnitzler's works. Without language to express the conflicting and rapidly changing feelings of the characters, the intensity of passion and the violent fluctuations of mood are portrayed by the exaggerated movements, postures, gestures, and facial expressions of mime, supported by music.

We do not know whether Schnitzler had also intended his companion pantomime, *The Transformation of Pierrot* ("*Die Verwandlung des Pierrot*") to be set to music. The piece was written in 1908 and never published separately. I have not been able to find any record of its ever having been performed. The central theme is a favorite of Schnitzler's: the contrast between the world of the theater, the realm of illusion, role-playing, and make-believe on the one hand, and ordinary life, the world of reality on the other. Katharina's romantic dreams of adventure, passion, and freedom from everyday responsibility are apparently fulfilled and subsequently shattered by Pierrot, the actor in a small amusement park theater, who constantly changes the parts he performs and transforms himself before our eyes into a variety of characters. The dream turns into a hallucinatory nightmare. In a central scene, we observe Pierrot in a play within the play (or more precisely a pantomime within a pantomime) stepping off his stage and out of his role into the "real" world. The make-believe audience is unaware of Pierrot's transformation.

The three one-act plays *The Puppeteer* (*Der Puppenspieler*), *The Gallant Cassian* (*Der tapfere Cassian*), and *The Great Puppet Show* (*Zum großen Wurstel*) form a cycle called *Marionettes*. *The Puppeteer* was written between 1901 and 1903, premiered at the Berlin Deutsches Theater, and is presented here for the first time in English translation. Georg is only a figurative puppeteer; he sees himself as a master manipulator, the piper who can make other people dance to his tune. The artist figure is obsessed with the notion that he can exercise creative power over human lives. He is the one who "pulls the strings." But in an ironic turnabout, the "puppets" whom he believes to be products of his imagination have taken on a life of their own. At the end, the artist is more lonely, more isolated, and less human than the ordinary people to whom he considered himself superior.

Cassian was written between 1902 and 1904, and premiered under the direction of Max Reinhardt at Berlin's Kleines Theater in 1904. Two years later, Oscar Straus used a slightly altered 1906 version as the libretto of his "Singspiel" *Der tapfere Kassian*, first performed at the Stadttheater in Leipzig in 1909. Previous English translations of the play were published in 1914 and 1922.

Unlike *The Puppeteer*, in which the characters are human beings, *The Gallant Cassian* is written for mechanical puppets. To the best of my knowledge, however, it was never performed as a puppet play, nor is there any indication that Schnitzler ever had such an intention. *The Puppeteer* shows people of flesh and blood being manipulated like wooden puppets on strings; *Cassian* shows puppets being portrayed by human actors. To an even greater extent than in the pantomime plays, the unreality of the medium serves to emphasize the unreality of the romantic dreams of grand passion and adventure. The rapidity of mood changes, the swiftness of the action, the easy rejection of humdrum, ordinary life all have mechanical qualities, which are intended to be representative of similar features in reality.

The third play of the cycle, *The Great Puppet Show*, was written in the years 1901-04 and originally called *Marionetten*. It saw its first performance under this title at the Berlin cabaret "Überbrettl" in 1904. In 1906 it was premiered under its new title *Zum großen Wurstel* at the Lustspiel Theater in the "Prater," the Viennese amusement park in which the play takes place — as does the central scene of the pantomime *Pierrot*. The former title *Marionetten* was now given to the collection of the three one-act plays which deal with the puppet theme. The entire cycle was first performed at the Vienna Deutsches Volkstheater in 1912; almost all subsequent productions followed the practice of showing all three plays in one evening. This volume presents *The Great Puppet Show* for the first time in English translation.

This play not only echoes the location of a scene in *Pierrot*, but also the device of a play within a play and the blurring of the boundary between reality and illusion. To be sure, there is nothing original about the idea that the world is a stage on which human beings act out their assigned parts. This concept is basically Baroque in origin, and is expressed by Calderón in *El gran teatro del mundo* and of course by Shakespeare. It is also very much part of the Austrian literary tradition. But Schnitzler uses the theme very effectively through the medium of the puppet play. The "real" stage actually shows three stages. One is an old-fashioned Punch-and-Judy style theater in which hand puppets perform pantomime battles to the delight of the children in the audience. A second one gives us a brief glimpse into a music hall performance intended strictly for light amusement. The third, central stage is a marionette theater which combines comedy and tragedy, entertainment and enlightenment — a grotesque mixture to which Schnitzler gave the name "burlesque." The play within a play enacted on this marionette stage by live actors contains motifs which parody themes from Schnitzler's own dramas *Liebelei, Der Schleier der Beatrice*, and *Der Ruf des Lebens* ("*The Call of Life*"). The characters not only include parodies of Schnitzlerian prototypes such as the "sweet young thing" or the very modern anti-hero, but also Death in the guise of Punch (or Punch in the guise of Death) and a Commentator called "*Raisonneur*" who foreshadows the stage manager of Wilder's *Our Town*.

In addition, members of the "audience" on stage, as well as in the actual audience in the theater interrupt and comment on the performance. This "audience" includes characters from plays by Schnitzler's writer-friends Hermann Bahr (*The Master*) and Richard Beer-Hofmann (*The Count of Charolais*). Both the director/manager/barker of the marionette theater and the "author" of the play within the play participate in the action, to add to the confusion. These are devices reminiscent of Tieck's Romantic version of *Der gestiefelte Kater* ("*Puss in Boots*").

The fictitious marionette characters take on a life of their own. The Unknown Man not only cuts their visible strings but also the invisible strings of the on-stage members of the "audience," who are revealed to be as "unreal" as the puppets which were also portrayed by actors. Finally, when The Unknown Man threatens to sever the strings of the spectators in the theater as well, it is the reality of our own existence which is called into question. But The Unknown Man leaves — fortunately — without carrying out his threat. Thereupon, the marionette-actors and the human being-actors on stage come back to "life" and the play begins all over again — anticipating Max Frisch's play *Die chinesische Mauer* ("*The Great Wall of China*") in which "real" people and characters from history, legend, and fiction also intermingle on stage and which also concludes with its own beginning in a never-ending cycle. In some ways, this "non-ending" also anticipates the conclusion of Brecht's drama *Der gute Mensch von Sezuan* ("*The Good Woman of Setzuan*") in which Brecht, in the person of the actor portraying The First God, confesses his inability to come up with a definitive answer and urges the audience to find it own conclusion.

Schnitzler wrote an outline of *Paracelsus* in 1894. Not until 1897-98 did he return to and complete his draft. The play first appeared in print in the periodical *Cosmopolis*. It was published in 1899 together with *Der grüne Kakadu* and *Die Gefährtin* ("*The Helpmate*"). The first performance of these three one-act plays took place at the Vienna Burgtheater on March 1 of that year. An English translation was published in 1913. I have not found any record of an American performance.

The title character is a historical figure who was also the hero of Browning's 1835 narrative poem by the same name. Philippus Aureolus Paracelsus Theophrastus von Hohenheim, known as "Bombastus," was born on December 17, 1493 in a small town in Switzerland, traveled widely, and died on September 23, 1541 in Salzburg, where a statue in his honor was erected in 1752. He was a very well-known physician, alchemist, pharmacist and theosopher who lectured and wrote in German (rather than in Latin) on medical subjects, rejected the traditional views of Galen, introduced chemical agents as medications, and was famous for his "miracle cures."

Schnitzler's interest in psychoanalysis is well known, and his insights were acknowledged by Sigmund Freud. As a young physician, he was also fascinated by the work of Friedrich (or Franz) Anton Mesmer whose theory of "animal magnetism" led him to attempt to treat patients by means of hypnosis, with which Schnitzler himself also experimented. Both Freud and Schnitzler were introduced to Mesmer's theories by a prominent Viennese physician, Dr. Josef Breuer.

Paracelsus is portrayed in the play as an early practitioner or therapeutic hypnotism. At the same time, he also (like Freud and Schnitzler himself) attaches a great deal of significance to dreams. In addition, like Georg in *The Puppeteer*, he admits that he plays with human beings. And just like Georg, he cannot always control the consequences of the thoughts he implants in others. (In a strange way, his methods foreshadow those of the evil hypnotist Cipolla in Thomas Mann's short story *Mario and the Magician*.)

But most importantly, Schnitzler's Paracelsus is a moral relativist for whom there exists no certainty, no truth, no permanence, no genuine knowledge either of the self or the world outside ourselves. The past as well as the future are abstractions; only the impressions of the moment are real. Here Schnitzler echoes the views of the physicist and phenomenologist Ernst Mach whose works strongly influenced him and his fellow impressionistic writers of the Young Vienna School. The ultimate conclusion is expressed by Paracelsus in his parting words: "We always play. Wise is the man who knows it." His conviction that all we ever do is play must be understood in terms of the double meaning of the German word "*spielen.*" On the one hand, it refers to playing a game; on the other hand, it carries the sense of playacting, pretending, role playing. Life is seen as a meaningless game in which all of us act out our ever-changing roles.

The Green Cockatoo is Schnitzler's best-known and most frequently performed one-act play. Written in 1898, its Berlin premiere scheduled for the same year was banned by the censor. A somewhat cut version was produced at the Vienna Burgtheater in 1899, but lasted only for six performances before the censor intervened again. Schnitzler's treatment of the French aristocracy was apparently too harsh to be allowed in public. In the same year, the work (in its entirety) was published together with the one-act plays *Paracelsus* and *Die Gefährtin*. Even in the 1930s, only the cut version was shown on the Viennese stages. During the Hitler years, of course, Schnitzler was not performed in Germany and Austria at all. Not until after World War II did Heinrich Schnitzler direct the complete *Cockatoo* at the Theater in der Josephstadt in Vienna. In 1956, Richard Mohaupt used the play as a libretto for an opera by the same title. Text and music were published in 1958; in the same year, the work was pre-miered in Hamburg. English translations and American produc-tions of *The Green Cockatoo* were discussed earlier in this essay.

At first glance, *The Green Cockatoo* looks like a typical nat-uralistic play of the period. The stage setting is described in great detail and the style of the dialogue is realistic. It is also one of the few Schnitzler dramas which is very specifically placed both geographically and historically: Paris on the eve of the fall of the Bastille, July 14, 1789, in a tavern frequented both by low-life types and members of the French aristocracy. But the appearance of realism is deceptive. The theme of the play is neither political nor sociological. Instead, Schnitzler is concerned precisely with the deceptive appearance of reality, the uncertain boundaries between substance and illusion, truth and make-believe, *Sein und Schein* (being and seeming). Everyone is putting on an act, playing a role. The apparent gangsters are actors, but when a real criminal tries to join the troupe, he fails to act convincingly. The aristocrats play games of deception and betrayal. Henri's make-believe fiction turns out to be more true than he realized. The innkeeper Prospère is actually a theater manager and director, but Henri's illusion is so convincingly portrayed that even Prospère can no longer distinguish it from reality. As Rollin says, "all apparent differences are suspended." Things are true only at the moment when they are spoken. All of life is only a theatrical performance.

The seven one-act plays in this volume were written during little more than a decade of the *fin-de-siècle*, the turn of the nineteenth century. Although they are almost a hundred years old, they are anything but old-fashioned. Instead, in many ways they anticipate late twentieth century trends in modern drama. In these and other plays by Schnitzler, we find the antecedents of Beckett's and Ionesco's theater of the absurd, of Pinter's and Dürrenmatt's black comedies. And the inability to distinguish between reality and illusion, the figure of the actor as the prototype of the role-playing individual, the stage as the fictional mirror of an equally deceptive life, all these themes of Schnitzler's reappear in plays like Pirandello's *Six Characters in Search of an Author* or *Henry IV*, Genet's *Balcony*, or Tom Stoppard's *Rosencrantz and Guildenstern Are Dead*. Like his contemporaries Chekhov and Ibsen, Arthur Schnitzler is seen today as a seminal forerunner of many twentieth-century dramatic trends. More and more it has become apparent that the judgment of *Theater Arts Monthly's* obituary was both inaccurate and premature.